THE

WOMAN

GOD

LOVES

EDE CHUKWUEMEKA

DEDICATION

THIS IS BOOK IS DEDICATED TO WOMANHOOD

PREFACE

It is written that God said, let us make man in our own image and likeness and let them have dominion over the fish of the sea and over the fowl of the air, and over the cattle, and over all the earth, and over every creeping thing that creep upon the earth. So God created man in his own image, in the image of God created he him; male and female created he them and called them man.

There were standards that God set for man as specie called by His name and man, is expected to live by these standards. I know that you know, that when the word of God stated that God made man in His own image and likeness, it meant that He made man to be like Him in all ramifications. Therefore man can say, I am perfect because God is perfect, I am holy because God is holy, I am truthful because God is truthful, I am spirit because God is Spirit, etc.

The Bible says that after the Lord God created man, He said, "It is not good that man should be alone; I will make him a help meet. And the Lord God caused a deep sleep to fall upon Adam and he slept and He took one of his ribs and closed up the flesh". It was from the rib that God took from man that He made a woman. When He brought her unto the man, the man said, "This now is the bone of my bones and the flesh of my flesh, she shall be called Woman because she was taken out of Man". They both stayed in the Garden naked and they were not ashamed.

It was the woman that the serpent met at the fall of man in the Garden of Eden. The Bible story says that the serpent was more subtle than any beast of the field which the Lord God had made and it took advantage of the weakness in the woman by encouraging her to take of the fruit the Lord God had instructed them not to eat and ate from it before giving to her husband and he also ate.

After what happened between God and man in the story of creation and the failure of man to keep the dominion God granted him, God never stopped to love the woman in a special way. He told Abraham to listen to his wife Sarah and chase Hagar away. Then He went to Hagar and her son in the desert, to save them.

God visited Sarah in her old age and she conceived. He remembered Rachel and she got pregnant. He answered Hannah, saved Rehab the prostitute, used Esther, Ruth, the widow of Zerepherth, Elizabeth, Mary the mother of Jesus, Mary Magdalene, the Samaritan woman and He must remember you. Yes you.

When they brought the woman caught in adultery to Him, Jesus refused to look up for some time because He knew what men were doing. That woman was caught with a man, but he was not there and Jesus knew that those who brought the woman were sinners. He raised his head and said to them, let him who has no sin, throw the first stone. That was not what they wanted to hear.

Jesus speaking in the book of Matthew said, it had been said whosoever shall put away his wife, let him give her a writing of divorcement but I say to you, that whosoever shall put away his wife, saving for the cause of fornication, causes her to commit adultery and whosoever shall marry her that is divorced commits adultery. Matthew 5: 31-32

Also in Mark chapter 10, the Pharisees came to him, and asked him, "Is it lawful for a man to put away his wife?" He answered and said to them, "What did Moses command you?" And they said, Moses ordered us to write a bill of divorcement and to put her away. Jesus answered and said to them, it was for the hardness of your heart that he wrote you this precept.

He continued speaking and said; that from the beginning of the creation God made them male and female. And added, "For this cause shall a man leave his father and mother and cleave to his wife and they twain shall be one flesh: so then they are no more twain, but one flesh. What therefore God hath joined together, let not man put asunder". Mark 5: 2-9.

Are you a woman? God loves you more than you can ever imagine and He wants to love you, even more. That is why this book is for you. I want you to understand that when it comes to God, love is absolutely reciprocal. If you truly love Him, He must truly love you back unconditionally. The Bible says that you should not be deceived; God knows those who are His. You are one of His and He is today reaching out His hands in love to you.

Please don't mind my repeating some names of the women of the Bible in this book. These names were repeated over and over again, because they all had some exceptional qualities that fell into each chapter. I used them as my prototypes in explaining the woman God loves and you will enjoy it as you read.

CONTENT

CHAPTER ONE: Giving Woman

CHAPTER TWO: Praying Woman

CHAPTER THREE: Believing Woman

CHAPTER FOUR: Faithful Woman

CHAPTER FIVE: Loving Woman

CHAPTER SIX: Caring Woman

CHAPTER SEVEN: Obedient Woman

CHAPTER EIGHT: Wise Woman

CHAPTER NINE: Courageous Woman

CHAPTER TEN: Discerning Woman

CHAPTER ELEVEN: Interactive Woman

CHAPTER ONE: Giving Woman

AND GOD SAID, BEHOLD, I HAVE GIVEN YOU EVERY HERB BEARING SEED, WHICH *IS* UPON THE FACE OF ALL THE EARTH, AND EVERY TREE, IN THE WHICH *IS* THE FRUIT OF A TREE YIELDING SEED; TO YOU IT SHALL BE FOR MEAT. AND TO EVERY BEAST OF THE EARTH, AND TO EVERY FOWL OF THE AIR, AND TO EVERYTHING THAT CREEPETH UPON THE EARTH, WHEREIN THERE *IS* LIFE, *I HAVE GIVEN* EVERY GREEN HERB FOR MEAT: AND IT WAS SO.

Once giving is mentioned, the first place of thought is always money and most women love to save money. But giving goes beyond money. It includes giving food, assistance, support, your ears, your hands, your time, your efforts, your words, your attitude and your character, etc. Giving is a very important department in the Kingdom of God.

Giving is so important, that God started from the beginning of creation to show it. In the book of Genesis which is the first book of the Bible, verses 27 to 30, shows God in giving action. It is written, that He created them, male and female and gave them everything from fruitfulness to dominion and foods for their living and enjoyment. He made them in His own image and likeness; hence He expects them to be like Him in all things including giving.

The woman, God loves is therefore the woman that gives without compulsion. This woman does not need to be pushed before she gives. She has it in her character, to give in all circumstances. This character of giving is made to be inherent in the woman God created. That is, women are carriers of the gift of giving. However some suppress this gift because of certain circumstances surrounding their lives or they were taught and learnt not to be givers from one person or the other. This teacher might be family or friends.

God is not interested in whatever may be your reason for not giving, because He too has every reason not to give. But He ignored them all and has kept giving without limitations. So the woman, that has a reason for not giving no matter what such reason might be, is not a friend of God. God's word confirms that He hates anyone who is in a position to give but does not do so.

This therefore goes to confirm, that the person who is in a position to give and does so is a friend of God and God loves His friends. You exist as a person because of the gifts of God. The Bible says that He gave his son Jesus Christ, to die in your place and He expects you to die in the place of another person by constantly giving, without limitations.

Your expectations can never be met until you meet the expectation of others who you are better than. Think of it, you think you are poor but there are people who are poorer than you are. Whatever situation you are in, there are many people who are in worst situations.

Looking into the scriptures, you will see a lot of women who gave and were blessed by God. Let us start with Sarah the wife of Abraham. In Genesis chapter 16 from verses 1-3, the Bible tells Sarah's story as a woman who did not give birth to a child until her old age. She did something that is rear for a woman to do.

She had a handmaid, an Egyptian, whose name was Hagar. Sarah said to Abraham, since I am restrained from bearing: I pray you to go to my maid; it may be that I may obtain children by her. And Abraham did as she had advised him by sleeping with Hagar the

Egyptian maid of Sarah, who she gave her to her husband Abraham to be his wife.

This is unbelievable. A woman gave another woman to her own husband? Though this is very difficult to do, Sarah did it because she felt, that she owed her husband the duty of child bearing which she could not perform due to her condition at that time. All she thought about was how to make her husband happy and God did not disappoint her at the end of the day. She later became pregnant and gave birth to her son Isaac according to the promise of God to her husband.

Peter writing in the book of 1 Peter chapter 3 verses 3-6, by the inspiration of the Holy Spirit confirmed his attraction to this exceptional woman who God loved dearly and used her as an example for other women to follow. He advised whoever is adorning not let it be of outward adorning, of plaiting the hair, and of wearing of gold, or of putting on of apparel.

He stated that beauty should be from the heart, in that which is not corruptible, even the ornament of a meek and quiet spirit, which is in the sight of God of great price. For after this manner in the old time the holy women also, who trusted in God, adorned themselves being in subjection to their own husbands. He added that Sarah obeyed Abraham, calling him lord and every woman is a daughter of Sarah, as long as she does well and is not afraid with any amazement.

One may guess that it was Sarah's story that Rachel the wife of Jacob heard and decided to toll her path. According to Genesis chapter 30 verses 4, she also gave her maid servant to her husband and he slept with her. Her sister Leah who was also Jacob's wife, did the same thing in verse 9. She also gave her own maid servant to her husband and he slept with her. These stories portrays what the ordinary person, would see as odd but it was destiny being fulfilled.

God had predestined Jacob to give birth to twelve children and He had arranged it, for his wives to do what they did. If these two sisters who were the wives of Jacob had not given their maid servants to their husband, God would have probably made an alternative arrangement. But things worked according to the original plan saving God time.

The Bible says, that God remembered Rachel and she conceived. It was through that pregnancy, that she gave birth to Joseph who became a prime minister in Egypt and saved the lives of the children of Israel during the famine of that time.

I have heard the story of a 21st century woman who had no child for her husband. She was the sister of very rich men and so, she did everything to make her husband happy. She will give him money and buy whatever she thought, he needed. Their marriage was looking peaceful but it was not. This man at a time made a plan with his friend and went to marry another woman who, he kept outside and she had a baby for him.

At a time, his first wife heard about the other woman through gossip and called her husband for talks. She told her husband everything she had heard and asked him to bring that other woman and her baby home. The husband could not believe it and was afraid to comply with his wife's request.

After sometime and serious persuasions however, he went and brought the other woman and her child. His first wife was so happy to live with them in the same house and acted as a mother to the second woman and her child. Before she knew it as time went on, she too became pregnant and gave birth to a baby boy. The second wife had come with a baby girl.

Solomon wrote that there is a time and a season for everything under the sun and I add here that God has the master plan for them all. When it was time for Isaac the son of Abraham to get married, the choice of

Rebekah was made by heaven and she was programmed to play a part, to bring it to pass. Her part was very simple, she was to meet a stranger and give to him whatever he asked from her. You can see with me why it is very important for the giving character in you, to be awake and responsive.

Rebekah did not know what was going to happen on that day, but she was equipped with the ability she needed to face it. Her story is very interesting as we read it from the Bible. Abraham's servant had taken an oath to bring a wife for Isaac from his father's kinsmen and he did not want to fail. So he prayed a prayer for help from the Lord, asking God to help him, to succeed speedily.

The prayer of the servant of Abraham is recorded in Genesis chapter 24. He told the Lord, that He stood by the well of water and the daughters of the men of the city come out to draw water. Then he requested that the damsel to whom he said, "Let down thy pitcher, I pray thee, that I may drink; and she shall say, Drink, and I will give thy camels drink also: let the same be she *that* thou hast appointed for thy servant Isaac; and thereby shall I know that thou hast showed kindness unto my master".

That was a serious request. It's only the truly faithful, that can pray that way. What happened next is unbelievable. Before he had done speaking, Rebekah who was born to Bethuel, son of Milcah, the wife of Nahor, Abraham's brother, came out, with her pitcher on her shoulder. She was very fair, a virgin, who no man had known.

As she went down to the well, filled her pitcher and came up, the servant of Abraham ran to meet her and asked her for a drink. She was quick to say, drink, my lord. She hasted, let down her pitcher to her hand and gave him drink. After she had done that, she told the man, that she will draw water for his camels also, so they can drink. She again hasted and emptied her pitcher into the trough, and ran to the well to draw water, and drew for all the camels.

The answer to the servant's prayer surprised him. Even though he was the one that said the prayer, he did not expect an answer to come as quickly as it did. God answered him with an extra ordinary speed and this made him wonder but God knew he was coming and He (God) had set everything in order, waiting his arrival. Rebekah was the right answer to the servant's prayer, so she wasted no time as soon as he asked her for a drink. God is a master planner.

Rebekah's heart had been positioned for a time like that and she was willing to comply fully with the leading of the Spirit of God. It was not the first day, she gave. I am sure she was a habitual giver and so it was not difficult for her to do what she was used to. She had told herself, that it was better to be in the place of giving than to be in the place of receiving. Her release of what she had in her hands was fast and smooth showing a heart filled with the presence of God Almighty.

Something deep inside her, must have told her that some day she will marry someone who is very rich and that she will be giving without looking back. She used to tell herself, that she and her husband would build an orphanage, visit the sick and give aids to so many people.

This was why, when she heard the servant of Abraham, say that God had blessed his master, she said yes! That's where I am going and once her family asked her, if she was going with the servant of Abraham, she answered and said yes. She was ready to be used by God. God loves every woman like Rebekah.

1 Samuel 1 tells the story of Hannah. This woman was married to a husband who had another wife. The story says, that Hannah had no children but her husband's other wife had children and used it to provoke her. The

situation did put Hannah in a bitterness of heart, but that was not God's plan for her.

God had set this Hannah to be the mother of Samuel, who God wanted to use for His own purpose and He (God) was waiting for her to be prepared to do an extra ordinary thing and something in her kept triggering her to move towards that direction. Reading from verses 9-11, the Bible say that Hannah rose up and went to pray after they had eaten and drank in Shiloh.

Now Eli the priest sat on a seat by a post of the temple of the Lord and he noticed Hannah while she prayed. She was in bitterness of soul and prayed to the Lord and she wept sore. She made a vow to the Lord of hosts, saying that if the Lord will indeed look on her affliction and remember her and not forget her but give her a man child, then she will give him back to the Lord all the days of his life and no razor shall come on his head.

Hannah came out and made a statement. She said to God, give me a son and I will give him back to you. My guess here is that God was not surprised by that statement. He had been prompting her to do what she did. Hannah was an instrument God had set apart for a purpose, but she was busy with the thoughts of having a son for herself and her husband which was not what God wanted.

God wanted her to have a son for Him and that son was Samuel. It was the vow she vowed that opened the hands of God who was willing to give her more than just one child but He wanted her to first give Him her first.

Elkanah, Hannah's husband did not argue with her when she told him about the vow she vowed to God before she got pregnant and her sincere willingness to fulfill it by giving the child to serve in God's house. My thought is that God had also touched Elkanah's heart to comply with his wife. Hannah's gift to God was received with gladness and after Samuel was received to do His work, God responded to Hannah by giving her other children for herself and her husband.

The giving woman is always a winning woman. In 1 Samuel 25, Abigail the wife of Nabal came to light with her ability to save her husband who David had marked for death with his entire family. Abigail was told what happened when her husband received visitors from David. The purpose of the visit was to ask for favor from Nabal who was a very prosperous man but he refused to give even though he was asked to give anything he felt was good in his eyes.

His wife Abigail being a giver was quick to make arrangements and went off to meet David and his men. That action of Abigail was what saved her family. David had decided that they will all die by the sword before the next morning, but Abigail came on time to stop the coming disaster. David had already taken his sword and was on his way to Nabal's house with four hundred men.

He was going to wipe Nabal and his family out of the face of the earth, but Abigail made haste and took two hundred loaves, two bottles of wine, five sheep ready dressed, five measures of parched corn, an hundred clusters of raisins, two hundred cakes of figs and laid them on asses. She told her servants to on before me while she came behind him and she did not tell her husband Nabal.

As she rode on the ass and came down by the covert on the hill, she saw David and his men come down against her and she met them. David had said, surely in vain have I kept all that this fellow hath in the wilderness, so that nothing missed out of all that was his but he has paid me evil for good. David swore by God not to leave any that is Nabal's by the morning light. He was going to kill any that pissed against the wall.

24

When Abigail saw David, she was fast and got off the ass,. She fell before David on her face and bowed herself to the ground. She fell at his feet and said, "Upon me, my lord, upon me let this iniquity be: and let thine handmaid, I pray thee, speak in thine audience, and hear the words of thine handmaid".

She called her husband a man of Belial, making reference to the meaning of his name. She called David my lord and explained to him, that she did not see the young men he sent to their house when they came. She pleaded with him saying, as the Lord lives and David's soul lives, seeing the Lord had withheld him from coming to shed blood, and from avenging himself by his own hand, he should let his enemies and those that seek to do evil to him, be as Nabal.

Then she showed him the things which she had brought and told him, to receive them for the young men that followed him. She asked for his forgiveness of the trespass of herself and her family, telling David that the Lord will certainly make him a sure house; because he fought the battles of the Lord and evil was not found in him all his days.

Abigail had prepared herself very well in a hurry and David was pleased with her approach. He received from her hand all, that she brought and asked her to go to her house in peace. David also said, I have heard your voice and have accepted your person. After the whole incident, Nabal died and David sent to take Abigail as his own wife because he saw the good woman in her. She loved her family more than anything and she could give anything, to save them.

Another woman of interest is the widow of Zerephath in 1 king 17. This widow had prepared herself with her son, to die because they had little to eat and there was famine in the land. Suddenly, a visitor she never knew appeared from nowhere and asked her for a drink. The Bible says that she turned to go and get the water for this stranger. See the story as the Bible narrated it from verses 8-16.

When this stranger the poor dying woman did not know, told her that the Lord had said it was well, she agreed and went to do what he asked from her. Tell me how she knew that the man was not lying? Now it was not about what the man said again. This woman called herself a sinner but she was a giver and God had seen the trouble that was coming to her. God knew that her son will die and He knew how the woman had been so good and kind even though she was a poor widow. So He had sent Elijah to her, for him to help her in the event of the death of her son.

See how the Bible completed the woman's story from verses 17-24. The son of the woman, the mistress of the house, fell sick; and his sickness was so sore, that there was no breath left in him. And she said unto Elijah, What have I to do with you, O thou man of God? Art thou come unto me to call my sin to remembrance, and to slay my son? And he said to her, give me your son. He took the boy out of her hands and carried him up into a loft, where he stayed and laid him on his own bed.

He then cried to the Lord and said, "O LORD my God, hast thou also brought evil upon the widow with whom I sojourn, by slaying her son"? Then he stretched himself on the child three times as he cried to the Lord. He said, "O LORD my God, I pray thee, let this child's soul come into him again". So the Lord heard the voice of Elijah and the soul of the child came back to him again. Once the child was revived, Elijah took him and handed him to his mother. And the woman said to him, now by this I know that you are a man of God, and that the word of the Lord in the mouth is truth.

There is no doubt, that God loves the woman that gives. This widow was poor, but she even gave at the risk of her life and that of her son. She did not know what her giving was going to do for her. That's why the Bible says that we should sow without with-holding the hand because we do not know which of the seed, would germinate and bear fruit for us. It may be the first, the middle or the last.

According to 2 kings 4, from verses 8-11, there is a story of what happened to Elisha in Shunem. The bible says that there was a great woman who used to constrain Elisha to stay and eat bread in her house. The woman did not do it once, she did it always and the man of God would stay and eat each time he passed that way. As it went on, the woman one day said to her husband, let us make a room for this man of God so that he can come in to stay whenever he is here in Shunem. Although this woman was rich, she had to discuss her intention with her husband who accepted and they made the room which Elisha stayed in Shunem.

When they made the room for Elisha, he came there to stay on a particular day and he was pressed to ask question about the woman and what he could do for her. Her gifts had triggered the man of God, to seek how he could be of assistance to this wonderful woman.

The scripture states that Elisha told his servant to call the woman and when the woman stood before him, he directed his servant to ask her what she would want him to do for her. The question included talking to the king on her behalf but the woman did not want any of things that he offered. However, there was something the servant of Elisha discovered. The woman had no child, so verses 12 to 16 described what happened after that discovery.

Elisha told Gehazi his servant, to call the Shunammite. And when he had called her, she stood before him. He told Gehazi, to say to the woman, 'Behold, thou hast been careful for us with all this care; what is to be done for thee? Wouldest thou be spoken for to the king, or to the captain of the host?

And she answered, I dwell among mine own people. And he said, what then is to be done for her? And Gehazi answered, verily she hath no child, and her husband is old".

Elisha said to Gehazi, "Call her". When he had called her and she stood in the door, the man of God told her, that about the same season, according to the time of life, she shall embrace a son. And she said, No, my lord, you are a man of God, do not lie to your handmaid. But the woman eventually conceived, and bore a son at that season that Elisha had said to her, according to the time of life.

If the enemy had known the seed that the Shunammite woman had sown before the child came, he would not have tried to steal him. That child was the fruit of a seed sown into God's own hands. He cannot die and her mother knew it. So when it was reported to her, that the child had stopped breathing, she prepared herself and went off to meet Elisha. When she was asked if all was well, she confidently answered that it was well. Was it well? Yes it was well.

She knew her stand and would not shake even though she walked through the valley of the shadow of death. Her son came back to life to prove that God will never forsake His beloved. In the time of the famine, she left her country but when she came back, all her properties were restored to her because of the story of her encounter with the man of God. God had made the arrangement so that as the servant of Elisha was talking with the king, she will come in to confirm what God had done.

Many times, people look at their bad situations and count them as reasons for not giving. But God does not see it that way. If you are poor and do not give, you will not give even if you were rich. Giving starts from whatever position you are in life. There are no restrictions in giving, the rich and the poor can give. The truth is that, there is always someone, somewhere, that you are richer than. Quote me. Each time you see this person, you realize that your own life is better.

Look at this widow in the book of Luke 21 verses 1-4. The woman was poor to the ground, but she gave all she had in the offering. The rich were there too, but Jesus said that they gave out of their abundance and she gave out of her poverty. Jesus loved her from that very moment.

This woman may have been asking God for something very important to her. It could have been for her children or her grand children. So many things would have been the reason for what the woman did and God saw it. If she had thought about her poverty, she would not have been able to give such offering. She instead used her situation to call on positive change, to come her way. You could be better than this woman, but has never done what she did. It may be what that situation you have been praying for, is requesting from you. Go extra length and see.

Mary Magdalene was a friend of Jesus. The Bible described her as a woman who was demon possessed and was delivered by Jesus. She and her entire family became friends with Jesus. This Mary did something in Matthew chapter 26. Reading from verses 6-13, you will see how she took a bottle of an expensive perfume and pored, it on Jesus. The disciples, who were there, became mad. They said, why waste it? But Jesus answered them.

The response of Jesus ended with a promise which says that where ever the gospel is preached, what she had done will be remembered in memorial of her. She did something ordinary and got an extra ordinary result. Who would have thought about it? She may have been thinking of what she could give to Him but found nothing suitable, so she went for that bottle of expensive ointment. Jesus knew the worth of that ointment and He gave her value for her money.

What is too expensive for you to give to God for His work, to His people in need? There are women who value their gold and other ornaments more than anything on this planet earth. There are those who value their shoes, some, their wrist watches, others, their many other items that they cannot share talk more of giving out. What can you not give for God's sake? Whatever it is, has become your own God and you do not know it.

Let me talk about Tabitha who the Bible brought up in the book of Acts chapter 9. This woman had died, but instead of the people around to help plan for her burial, they made plan to go and invite Peter so that he can come and pray for her. Their intention was to bring her back to life because they felt, that she did not deserve to die. To these people, Tabitha was too good to die. She made cloths for the widows and when Peter came, they showed them to him.

One may ask, if Tabitha was not a human being that would die and be buried just like others? The answer to such question is yes; she is a human being who can die and she died. You may ask again, what then? And I will say, my thought is that she had an unfinished duty to perform on earth. You see, heaven records it every time she did alms giving and gave cloths to the widows. There is always a great joy in heaven each time she performs this function. So when the widows and all the other people she rendered help to, called upon God for her sake, their cries got to heaven and heaven responded because it has her record with which to make reference.

Peter was there, just at the right time. Heaven had willing given approval for answer to the prayers offered on that day in favor of this woman, not minding who took charge of it. If you were there and prayed for Tabitha, she would have risen just as she did when Peter prayed. You can become Tabitha in your own community, your environment or your area.

Think about it and receive the grace from God in Jesus name. Life is bought every day, one person, and one day at a time.

What God is looking for, is that woman who would take it upon herself to become a giving hand to the less privileged of this time. The word of God is clear on the rewards, which await you, when you take up the mantle and start in any little way that you can. The Lord knows your capacity as of today and whatever you give is recorded according to what you have. See Proverbs chapter thirty one, verses ten, twenty, fourteen and twenty nine as copied from the scriptures:

10 Who can find a virtuous woman? For her price *is* far above rubies.

20 She stretcheth out her hand to the poor; yea, she reacheth forth her hands to the needy.

14 She is like the merchants' ships; she bringeth her food from afar.

29 Many daughters have done virtuously, but thou excellest them all.

Note these verses as shown above. I want to pick out the points here carefully starting from verse twenty nine which says, many daughters have done virtuously but you excel over them all. I brought this verse in, to show that even though you do not think that you can measure yourself with the other daughters of God in the different areas of their callings, you can excel above them all when you stretch out your hand to the poor and reach out to the needy.

Imagine giving, joint with fulfilling other ministries? That is, you are a giver, a preacher and a lover. Fire must always fall anywhere you are and people shall wonder where you are coming from. It's a dangerous combination, hard to find anywhere. The enemy is always following you child of God, if you have this combination and he tries very hard to stop you. That is why the Bible says in 1 Peter 5, verse 8, "Be sober, be vigilant; because your adversary the devil, as a roaring lion, walketh about, seeking whom he may devour:"

The devil will try to devour your finances by every means possible, break your heart and make you cry but you have to put your trust in the Lord and become like mount Zion that can never be removed. When he comes, you don't run. You constantly remain in the same spot as a giver, knowing who you serve and continually position yourself in the place of confirming God's love for you. He never fails.

CHAPTER TWO: Praying Woman

> BE CAREFUL FOR NOTHING; BUT IN EVERYTHING BY PRAYER AND SUPPLICATION WITH THANKSGIVING LET YOUR REQUESTS BE MADE KNOWN UNTO GOD.

The power of prayer is not as a result of the person praying. Rather, the power resides in the God who is prayed to. The book of 1 John 5:14-15 tells us, "This is the confidence we have in approaching God: that if we ask anything according to his will, he hears us. And if we know that he hears us, whatever we ask we know that we have what we asked of him."

No matter the person praying, the passion behind the prayer or the purpose of the prayer, God answers prayers that are in agreement with His will. His answers are not always yes, but are always in our best interest. When we pray passionately and purposefully, according to God's will, He responds powerfully.

The word of God advised that we should remain instant in prayer, that is praying without ceasing. It warns that the end of all things is at hand and so we must be sober and watch through prayer. There are a lot of things that we cannot do without prayer. The list is so numerous.

Jesus in His time on earth often went up to the mountain alone to pray and continued there in prayer all night. You may now ask yourself, if the son of God continued in prayer all night, what about me?

We cannot access powerful prayer by using "magic formulas." Our prayers being answered is not based on the eloquence of our prayers. We don't have to use certain words or phrases to get God to answer our prayers.

In fact, Jesus rebuked those who pray using repetitions. He advised that when you pray, you should not keep on babbling like pagans, for they think they will be heard because of their many words. He said that we should not be like them, for our Father knows what we need before we ask him. See, (Matthew 6:7-8).

Prayer is communicating with God. All you have to do is make contact with God and go before Him with your petition or give Him thanks for answered prayers. Psalm 107:28-30 says, "Then they cried out to the LORD in their trouble, and he brought them out of their distress. He stilled the storm to a whisper; the waves of the sea were hushed. They were glad when it grew calm, and he guided them to their desired haven."

There is power in that little prayer you said. Do not see it as a waste of time when you go before God and make any request. God's help through the power of prayer is available for all kinds of requests and issues that you may present before Him. As Philippians 4:6-7 says, you should not be anxious about anything. But in everything, by prayer and petition, with thanksgiving, you should present your requests to God. And the peace of God, which transcends all understanding, will guard your heart and your mind in Christ Jesus.

If you need an example of a prayer, read Matthew 6:9-13. These verses are known as the Lord's Prayer, the prayer Jesus taught His disciples when they asked Him to teach them, how to pray. He taught them the things that should go into a Prayer worship; trust in God, requests, confession, protection, etc. Pray for these kinds of things, as you go to speak to God using your own words.

The Word of God is full of accounts describing the power of prayer in various situations. The power of prayer has overcome enemies (Psalm 6:9-10), conquered death (2 Kings 4:3-36), brought healing

43

(James 5:14-15), and defeated demons (Mark 9:29). God, through prayer, opens eyes, changes hearts, heals wounds, and grants wisdom (James 1:5).

The power of prayer should never be underestimated because it draws on the glory and might of the infinitely powerful God of the universe! Peter wrote in the book of 1 Peter 3 saying, "For the eyes of the Lord are over the righteous, and his ears are open unto their prayers: but the face of the Lord is against them that do evil".

With the understanding of Peter's writing above, Paul wrote in Ephesians 1:15-23, saying; that after he heard of the faith of the Ephesians in the Lord Jesus, and love to all the saints, he cease not to give thanks for them, making mention of them in his prayers. He asked the God of our Lord Jesus Christ, the Father of glory, to give them the spirit of wisdom and revelation in the knowledge of him.

So that the eyes of their understanding being enlightened; they may know what is the hope of His calling and what is the riches of the glory of His inheritance in the saints and the exceeding greatness of His power towards those who believe, according to the working of His mighty power, which He showed in Christ, when He raised Him from the dead and set Him at His own right hand in the heavenly places.

When the righteous prays, it touches God. He loves to be touched and you can touch Him through your life of prayer. The instruction in His word is that we should confess our faults to each other and pray for one another so that we may be healed. It adds that the effectual fervent prayer of the righteous does great wonders.

A woman, who can pray, is a dangerous instrument in the hands of God. God always loves such woman, dearly and answers her prayers. Luke told a story on the dedication of the child Jesus at the temple in the book of Luke 2.

In his story, he brought up a woman named Anna who he said was a widow for forty four years and during these years, she did not leave the house of God. She served God with prayer and fasting, night and day. You can read this story for yourself in verses 36 and 37 of Luke 2. This woman stayed in the temple all the period of her widowhood. Can you imagine how fervently she prayed?

Whenever there is need for prayer, women always pray their hearts out. They go extra lengths in other to show how important it is to them and how urgent they need things done. As you know, they are often too emotional, so they go to God with their cups of emotions full. The determination of a serious woman in anything she does can never be equaled and it is the same when she prays. She comes with full force to attack whatever stands against her until victory is assured.

Women, really know how to touch God. In a previous chapter of this book, you came across Hannah because I used as an example. The Bible says that this woman was bitter in her soul before she went to God, to pray. In this instance, God was touched. He asked the hosts of heaven, did you hear what that woman just said? That is exactly what God wants. Quick He said, prepare the boy and send him immediately. Heaven got to work, prepared Samuel and sent him to Hannah.

Women are phenomenal. She said, "Because I asked him of the Lord". That is thanks giving and God appreciates thanksgiving so much. Another thing that God appreciates, is keeping our vows. So many times, people go to God in their desperate situations and make vows that they do not keep. Hannah was different in this case. She made sure, that she kept her vow to the Lord by bringing the child to serve in the house of God.

She weaned Samuel and took him up with her, with three bullocks, one ephah of flour, and a bottle of wine and brought him to the house of the Lord in Shiloh. They slew a bullock and brought the child to Eli the priest and the woman told him who she was why she came.

She said; that she is the woman that stood by him there and prayed to the Lord for a child and the Lord answered the petition which she made to Him. Therefore also, she had lent him to the Lord; so that as long as the child lived he shall be lent to the Lord. Promise made, promise kept.

Hannah did not stop to pray a prayer of thanksgiving. The scripture shows in the same 1 Samuel but in chapter 2, that she continued to give God thanks. As a matter of fact, she thanked God with joy in her heart and rejoiced that she had fulfilled her promise to God. Look at her prayers in 1 Samuel 2: 1-10:

1 And Hannah prayed, and said; My heart rejoiceth in the LORD, mine horn is exalted in the LORD: my mouth is enlarged over mine enemies; because I rejoice in thy salvation. 2 There is none holy as the LORD: for there is none beside thee: neither is there any rock like our God. 3 Talk no more so exceeding proudly; let not arrogancy come out of your mouth: for the LORD is a God of knowledge, and by him actions are weighed.

4 The bows of the mighty men are broken, and they that stumbled are girded with strength. 5 They that were full have hired out themselves for bread; and they that were hungry ceased: so that the barren hath born seven; and she that hath many children is waxed feeble. 6 The LORD killeth, and maketh alive: he bringeth down to the grave, and bringeth up. 7 The LORD maketh poor, and maketh rich: he bringeth

low, and lifteth up. 8 He raiseth up the poor out of the dust, and lifteth up the beggar from the dunghill, to set them among princes, and to make them inherit the throne of glory: for the pillars of the earth *are* the LORD's, and he hath set the world upon them.

9 He will keep the feet of his saints, and the wicked shall be silent in darkness; for by strength shall no man prevail. 10 The adversaries of the LORD shall be broken to pieces; out of heaven shall he thunder upon them: the LORD shall judge the ends of the earth; and he shall give strength unto his king, and exalt the horn of his anointed.

Hannah prayed and cried. That is how to touch God. You can see that she received her request. As she was bringing victuals to the house of God, her heart was filled with joy and she was giving thanks with her mouth thereby fulfilling what is written in the word of God which says that it is out of the abundance of the heart, the mouth speaks.

Now let the woman in you, rise in prayer to God and touch the Lord. Cry to Him and be willing to do whatever it takes. Pay careful attention to what you are asking from Him and focus on what He might require from you. Before you make a vow to God, make sure it is what you shall be able to fulfill with joy in your heart and always remember to fulfill it.

The other woman that touched God through her prayer was Esther. This woman had become a queen in the land of her slavery and her uncle warned her, not to disclose her identity. But something came up, that needed her to play a role in order to save her people from destruction. She was supposed to meet with the king and she knew of the rules regulating such meeting and how dangerous it was for her to disobey that rule.

All the king's servants and the people of the king's provinces, do know, that whosoever, whether man or woman, shall come to the king into the inner court, who is not called there has one law and that is to put the person to death. Unless the king shall hold out, the golden scepter, to such person shall he/she live.

The above rule described by the Bible was an order of the palace of the king and no one had ever attempted to disobey it. But Esther had a very big challenge coming from her uncle who she loved and cared for. This uncle of hers had sent to tell her that she had to see the king and make supplication for her people. He added that even if she refused to help them, help will come from somewhere else and her own family will be destroyed.

It was a very difficult task for Esther to undertake, but she decided to take the risk. She therefore sent a quick response to her uncle in reply to his message and threat. She stated in her swift response, that she was willing to do what he requested her to do. She understood that no further argument was necessary at that point. Below is how the Bible recorded her response in the book of Esther chapter 4: 15-17;

15 Then Esther bade them return Mordecai *this answer*, 16 Go, gather together all the Jews that are present in Shushan and fast ye for me, and neither eat nor drink three days, night or day: I also and my maidens will fast likewise; and so will I go in unto the king, which *is* not according to the law: and if I perish, I perish. 17 So Mordecai went his way, and did according to all that Esther had commanded him.

The strength of her statement is breath taking. Fearlessly she said, "If I perish, I perish". She requested that the people fast while she and her maidens do the same. They all went into fasting for three days, night and day. The Bible recorded her result in Esther chapter 5: 1-3 shown below;

1 Now it came to pass on the third day that Esther put on her royal apparel, and stood in the inner court of the king's house, over against the king's house: and the king sat upon his royal throne in the royal house, over against the gate of the house. 2 And it was so, when

the king saw Esther the queen standing in the court, that she obtained favor in his sight: and the king held out to Esther the golden sceptre that was in his hand. So Esther drew near, and touched the top of the sceptre. 3 Then said the king unto her, what wilt thou, Queen Esther? And what *is* thy request? It shall be even given thee to the half of the kingdom.

Do you see that? Power came after she fasted and the king asked her, what her request was without remembering the rule that was set in his palace. He was even willing to give her, half of his kingdom. That is the power of prayer and fasting. Women these days are often filled with excuses on why they cannot do food fasting. Some may even dare to fast for weight loose but not for prayer purposes and some Pastors now charge fees for fasting for such women.

What a shame? Someone told me a story of a woman who was told that death was before her and she needed to go into fasting and prayer. This woman told the

Pastor, to fast for her because she was too busy. She was willing to pay money for another person to fast for her instead of her doing it by herself. Can you imagine that? The story ended sadly. She died in a road accident and that was the end of her busyness.

I hope you are not too busy? I hope you are the one who will face the challenge before you squarely, using prayer and fasting? There are issues facing you that would not leave until you can pray hard with fasting. Jesus in answering a question his disciples asked Him with regards to their inability to cast out a demon, said "This one cannot go except by prayer and fasting". He was not talking to men of God only, He was talking to His entire followers and you reading this book now, is one of them.

There was another woman who touched God. The Bible says that the woman was a Greek, a Syrophenician by nation. She came to Jesus and prayed to Him about her daughter who was sick and dying, but

Jesus did not answer her. His disciples even asked Him what He was doing with the woman and told Him to send her away, but the woman stayed and waited patiently.

If you have ever been in a desperate need, then you have seen God's response seem like it's coming too slowly. That is when patient is required mostly. This woman was desperately in need and she was not supposed to go to Jesus because her people were seen as idol worshippers. But there she was, seating before the son of God and making a demand.

The instant answer she received was not encouraging but the condition she came for needed attention. Below is how the Bible told the story in Matthew 15: 21-27:

21 Then Jesus went thence, and departed into the coasts of Tyre and Sidon. 22 And, behold, a woman of Canaan came out of the same coasts, and cried unto him, saying, Have mercy on me, O Lord, thou son of David; my daughter is grievously vexed with a

devil. 23 But he answered her not a word. And his disciples came and besought him, saying, send her away; for she crieth after us. 24 But he answered and said, I am not sent but unto the lost sheep of the house of Israel. 25 Then came she and worshipped him, saying, Lord, help me. 26 But he answered and said, it is not meet to take the children's bread, and cast it to dogs. 27 And she said, truth, Lord: yet the dogs eat of the crumbs which fall from their masters' table.

Can you see the answers she got in response to her request? Jesus first kept calm and did not say anything to her. Then after a while, He told her, that He did not come for people like her but still she did not go away. She kept praying and pleading. When Jesus in response to her indirectly called her a dog, she answered and said yes, I am a dog and dogs eat from the crumbs that fall from their master's table. This answer overwhelmed Jesus. He was touched instantly and His response showed it.

I can testify that this woman would not have left Jesus if He had not attended to her need. She knew who she was and was not ashamed to accept it before the Lord. She prayed without ceasing, until her prayer was answered. Are you like her? Do you think that you don't deserve to come before the Lord? Do you always see your faults when you kneel down to pray? Jesus is saying to you today, I laid them all on the cross. He said, "Come to me all you who are weary and heavy laden and I will give you rest".

Jesus loves you. He came into the world to seek and save sinners. He said that He did not come for the righteous, He came for sinners. This is why the sinner should be happy to come to Him freely, not being afraid to let Him know how you feel and what you want Him to do for you. He is ever willing and able to extend a hand of fellowship to anyone who comes to Him in humility of heart.

The Bible says that He is faithful and just to forgive your sin and cleans you from all unrighteousness. Once, you confess to Him, He forgives and forgets. He does not want you to keep reminding Him of any sin, He forgave. If you don't know He forgave you, know it from today that He forgave you that day you confessed to Him. Yes He forgave you, as soon as you confessed and promised not to go back to it again. It ended there.

God is not a man that he should lie. He does whatever He said, He would do. He said come let us reason together, if your sin be as scarlet as red, it shall be cleansed as white as snow. It is a promise that God made and He keeps it. So go to Him now. In this very moment, share whatever you think He should know with Him and let it go. Once you can share it with Him, forget about it and never let it bother you again. It is gone for good, you are forgiven and it is forgotten.

To encourage you, let me show you another story similar to the story of the Greek woman I have just shared. Jesus told a parable in the book of Luke chapter 18, about a widow who needed judgment against her adversary. In this parable, He stated that the judge did not listen to the widow at her first appeal but as the woman kept pressing him and did not stop coming, he was forced to listen to her. The scripture narrates the parable this way:

1 And he spake a parable unto them *to* this end, that men ought always to pray, and not to faint; 2 Saying, There was in a city a judge, which feared not God, neither regarded man: 3 And there was a widow in that city; and she came unto him, saying, Avenge me of mine adversary.

4 And he would not for a while: but afterward he said within himself, though I fear not God, nor regard man; 5 Yet because this widow troubleth me, I will avenge her, lest by her continual coming she weary

me. 6 And the Lord said, Hear what the unjust judge saith. 7 And shall not God avenge his own elect, which cry day and night unto him, though he bear long with them?

Can we start talking about something now? Okay, let us look at the story of another woman who touched God. She was simply referred to in the scripture as the woman with the issue of blood. This woman touched Jesus physically because she thought to herself, that touching Him would heal her of the sickness she suffered from for a long time. She stood on the way that Jesus was passing by and touched Him as she had purposed in her heart.

This woman was healed from her infirmity, instantly.

You too can also, touch Jesus physically today. He said in His word, that as long as you do it to the least of His brethren, you have done it to Him. So then, you must begin to make a move of touch. As you touch the sick, the poor and the needy, the blind and the lame, the widows and the orphans, you have touched Jesus. Reach out and hold somebody's hands now. That is another form of prayer that God loves and answers speedily.

God did not create you, to think only of yourself. You were created to think about everybody around you. You might ask, how can this be possible? It is possible, when you can pray. You pray for yourself and pray for others. The Spirit filled woman can pray better. When you do not know what to pray for, the Spirit begins to intercede for you through wordless groans and you will be able to touch every areas of your life, family, friends and brethren in the Spirit realm. Begin to pray in the Spirit now!

CHAPTER THREE: Believing Woman

> AND ALL THINGS, WHATSOEVER YE SHALL ASK IN PRAYER, BELIEVING, YE SHALL RECEIVE.

Belief is a very important aspect of true Christianity. The scripture says that all things are possible to them that believe. There are so many things in the Christian faith, that you cannot understand but yet you see yourself believing in them even though, you cannot even explain why you believe them.

Unbelief is totally disallowed for the true Christian believer. You must understand that you cannot receive anything from God unless you believe. Yet God can sometimes attempt to make the unbeliever change by showing some signs.

See what God Himself said in the book of Isaiah 43: 10-13:

10 Ye *are* my witnesses, saith the LORD, and my servant whom I have chosen: that ye may know and believe me, and understand that I *am* he: before me there was no God formed, neither shall there be after me. 11 I, even I, *am* the LORD; and beside me there *is* no saviour. 12 I have declared, and have saved, and I have showed, when *there was* no strange god among you: therefore ye *are* my witnesses, saith the LORD, that I am God. 13 Yea, before the day *was* I am he; and there is none that can deliver out of my hand: I will work, and who shall let it?

When the Lord sent Moses to the children of Israel, Moses refused to go because he believed that it would be difficult for him to convince the people that he had, heard from the Lord. He therefore made frantic efforts to make God understand his feelings and they discussed it at length as recorded in the book of Exodus 4: 1-9.

Before anything you do would succeed, it must all start with changing the belief of the recipients. Where there is unbelief, efforts are limited because those who are involved cannot be changed to conform with what has been made available to them. Until there is belief, every attempt to convince an individual or group of people is always futile.

It is even worst, when the recipient believed in something else before the coming of a new knowledge.

Several times, Jesus was faced with the challenge of unbelief of the people. The Jews came to him and asked Him how long He would make them doubt. They wanted to know if He was the Christ or not and they asked Him to tell them plainly. When this question was thrown to Him, He tried as much as He could, to answer them.

Jesus answered them, I told you and you believed not. The works that I do in my Father's name, they bear witness of me. But you believe not, because you are not of my sheep, as I said to you. My sheep hear my voice, and I know them, and they follow me: And I give unto them eternal life and they shall never perish nor shall any man take them out of my hand.

He continued and said, if I do not the works of my Father, believe me not. But if I do, though you believe me not, believe the works that you may know and believe that the Father is in me and I in him. And many resorted to him, and said, John did no miracle: but all things that John spake of this man were true.

His answers to them, was plain enough to explain everything thing but many still did not believe. He said my sheep hear my voice and I know them and they follow me. Then He added that even though they did not believe in Him to be who He claimed to be, they should believe the works of His Father, He had shown them in His Father's name. He explained that they should not believe Him, if the works He did were not His Father's work.

The same incident had happened in the book of John chapter 5. Unbelief of the Jews was on focus in this chapter of the Bible. What happened? On a Sabbath day, Jesus healed a sick man who had been ill for thirty eight years and the Jews did not accept it because to them, the Sabbath should be kept holy as God had commanded them through Moses. Jesus however, tried to explain things to them.

He said that if they had believed Moses, they would have believed Him because Moses wrote of Him. But if they believed not Moses' writings, they shall not believe His words. If you do not believe the writing of the Father, how can you believe the words of His son? God has given you His word through the scriptures. He therefore expects you, to believe in what is written and do them for your benefits.

You cannot serve God in unbelief because He totally disagrees with the unbeliever who has personal ideas on what to do, instead of calling on Him and asking for assistance. Many of them often ask for signs before they will believe just like the Jews did in the days of Jesus on earth. John 6 has one of such requests recorded from verses 28-30 and included here as follows;

28 Then said they unto him, what shall we do, that we might work the works of God? 29 Jesus answered and said unto them, this is the work of God that ye believe on him whom he hath sent. 30 They said therefore unto him, what sign showest thou then, that we may see, and believe thee? What dost thou work? 31 Our fathers did eat manna in the desert; as it is written, He gave them bread from heaven to eat. 32 Then Jesus said unto them, verily, verily, I say unto you, Moses gave you not that bread from heaven; but my Father giveth you the true bread from heaven.

Now look at that question in verse 28, "What shall we do that we might work the work of God"? Then Jesus answered them in the next verse and said that the work of God is to believe on Him whom He sent. Still they did not understand.

They went further to ask for sign although He had shown many signs and is still showing many more signs. Their argument was that their fathers eat bread in the desert. But see how Jesus explained it to them. He said that it was not Moses that gave the bread from heaven, it was God the Father, who gave the bred from heaven.

What Jesus was saying here, is that signs, miracles and wonders are not performed by the person who does the work of God. They are rather performed by God. So then, one should not depend on the man or woman of God, but on God who performs all miracles. The unbelievers cannot understand this, because their hearts are not opened.

It is the heart that is opened that; receives and believe. When the heart is shut in unbelief, it closes the eyes of the, would be recipient from seeing whatever is done and makes it impossible for this person to receive.

Jesus tried to be open to them because He understood what they were passing through. After speaking to them, they said to Him, Lord, evermore give us this bread. In verse 35 of the same chapter, Jesus said to them, "I am the bread of life: he that cometh to me shall never hunger; and he that believeth on me shall never thirst. He added in the following verse; "I said unto you, that ye also have seen me, and believe not". Verse 47 says, "Verily, verily, I say unto you, He that believeth on me hath everlasting life".

You can agree with me, that women are always quick to believe and the woman who believes can go to any length in her efforts to show that her heart is in whatever she believes. She will always follow her belief to a logical conclusion and also strongly resist any attempt by anyone or group trying to stop or limit her from following what she believes in.

The women always stand firm against all odds, because they believe. The scripture in Luke chapter 8, introduced some women who followed Jesus and ministered to Him out of their substance. It is recorded from verses 1-3 that as He went about the villages preaching and showing the glad tidings of the kingdom of God, these women which had been healed of evil spirits and infirmities, Mary called Magdalene, out of whom went seven devils, Joanna the wife of Chuza Herod's steward, Susanna, and many others, ministered to Him out of their substance.

It was from the list of these women that the people recorded in Luke chapter 24, who went very early in the morning to visit the grave of Jesus and found that the stone was rolled out, came. This record proves that they followed Jesus from the time they met Him to the time of His crucifixion and resurrection.

The women were also there, when He ascended. It also goes to tell, that they believed in Him as much as the Apostles did. The Bible recorded in this story, that it was still one of these women that went and told the Apostles about seeing the angels who told her that Jesus had resurrected. It was Mary Magdalene, Joanna, Mary the mother of James and other women that were with them, which told these things to the Apostles.

Another woman of interest, when it comes to belief, is Mary the mother of Jesus. This woman was exceptional. The story of her meeting with the angel of God in Luke chapter 1, is very interesting. Here was a young woman, going about her personal business. She was suddenly called by a man she didn't know and the approach of that man was not normal. He greeted her in a way she had never been greeted by anyone and it was very strange to her.

After the strange greeting, the angel started telling her that she will be pregnant. What? Mary must have thought to herself, but remained calm. She simply asked one question, "How will this be?" The strange man answered and said that she will be overcome by the Holy Spirit and the power from the highest shall overshadow her.

Do you understand this scene? Being overshadowed by Power from the highest? The ordinary person would ask another question and that would have been, "What do you mean by that?" But Mary did not ask any further questions. She was under the control of the Holy Spirit who had taken over and so she simply said, "Behold the handmaid of the Lord; be it unto me according to thy word. And the angel departed from her".

What a powerful response. Heaven noted it instantly and counted it for her. She believed all that the angel had told her and immediately prepared to go and visit Elizabeth who the angel also mentioned in his message. She did not go to see a prophet or a priest to tell the story of her encounter with the stranger and ask them to make enquiry for her from the Lord, if what she heard was true of false, she just believed.

The Bible recoded that upon her visit to Elizabeth, Elizabeth was filled with the Holy Spirit on hearing her greeting and the baby in her womb jumped. Remember that Mary merely met with a man she did not know, was an angel. Why all of a sudden did she become a carrier of the grace of God?

The answer is because she simply believed. It's important for you to understand, that she was carrying this grace long before the angel even visited her. Elizabeth made a statement in verses 45 of the same Luke chapter 1, shown here. It reads, "And blessed is she that believed: for there shall be a performance of those things which were told her from the Lord".

When you believe, there shall be a performance of the things you were told. God's word must perform the purpose for which He sent it. This is a promise from Him, for the believer who moves without fear and does not look back. You can understand from the story of Mary, that she was not afraid.

She had heard about God before then and even though she had not encountered Him, she believed that God is good.

She wanted Him to use her for whatever He had in mind and it happened to her according to her belief.

It was still Mary's belief, which moved her to bring about the miracle of turning water into wine at the marriage in Cana of Galilee. The Bible recorded it, as the beginning of miracles Jesus did and manifested His glory. The story says that she went to Jesus and told Him that they had run out of wine. Then Jesus in answering, showed, that He was not concerned about such matter at that time.

But Mary as a mother cannot forget the details of her encounter before the birth of Jesus. She believed that He only had to speak for something to happen and so she directed the servants to do whatever He told them to do. That is the character of a strong believer. They will never waiver, no matter the circumstances before them. Whether it looks good or bad, they continue to believe until the situation becomes ashamed of them and all that belongs to them.

In John chapter 11, Lazarus was sick and his sisters believing in the power of healing sent a message to inform Jesus. The scripture states that they told him, that the one

He loved was sick. Their belief was that He would rush to them and lay hands on their brother to get well, but Jesus did not go to them until their brother died.

You can imagine how these women felt. The one they trusted on had disappointed them. Now, not only was their brother dead, he had been laid in the grave and so their belief had suffered a setback. See what happened when Jesus came after four days. Read below, verses 20-26:

20 Then Martha, as soon as she heard that Jesus was coming, went and met him: but Mary sat *still* in the house. 21 Then said Martha unto Jesus, Lord, if thou hadst been here, my brother had not died. 22 But I know, that even now, whatsoever thou wilt ask of God, God will give *it* thee. 23 Jesus saith unto her, Thy brother shall rise again.

24 Martha saith unto him, I know that he shall rise again in the resurrection at the last day. 25 Jesus said unto her, I am the resurrection, and the life: he that believeth in me, though he were dead, yet shall he live: 26 And whosoever liveth and believeth in me shall never die. Believest thou this?

Martha's answer showed it all. The death of her brother affected her, but there were still signs that she believed. She had said to Jesus, if you had been here my brother would not have died. She added that she knew that even then, whatever Jesus would ask of God, will be given Him. By this, Jesus must have thought that's okay and felt her belief was intact because He told her, that her brother shall rise again.

But notice the quick turn in her next speech. She responded with talk about resurrection at the last day. This was enough to give Jesus, signal that all was not well. So He quickly told her, that He is the resurrection and life. He went further to explain to her, that belief in Him was life and asked her a question to bring her back. But I think she was too devastated, to reason properly because her answer left the question. She said something different as recorded in verses 27-28 below.

27 She saith unto him, Yea, Lord: I believe that thou art the Christ, the Son of God, which should come into the world. 28 And when she had so said, she went her way, and called Mary her sister secretly, saying, The Master is come, and calleth for thee.

There was no hiding for the crack on the wall. Martha's belief had cracked. She left and went to call her sister. This could happen to you, but there is a lesson to be learnt here. Jesus knew what happened to her and He needed to reverse it immediately, to set her back on her feet. So as soon as she returned to Him again towards the end of this story with her belief not yet repaired, Jesus began to work on her.

He commanded, that the stone covering Lazarus grave should be taken off, but Martha tried to give an excuse as to why she felt the stone should not be rolled away. However Jesus knowing that what would happen, when the stone is rolled away would help to revive her belief in Him, made an encouraging statement recorded in verses forty of John chapter eleven in answer to her.

Read this with me starting from verses thirty eight to forty:

38 Jesus therefore again groaning in himself cometh to the grave. It was a cave, and a stone lay upon it. 39 Jesus said, Take ye away the stone. Martha, the sister of him that was dead, saith unto him, Lord, by this time he stinketh: for he hath been dead four days. 40 Jesus saith unto her, said I not

unto thee, that, if thou wouldest believe, thou shouldest see the glory of God?

What Jesus meant when He said, said I not to you that if you should believe, you will see the glory of God, is that He has commanded you. He wants you to obey everything He commanded and surely He is with you always, to the very end of the age. If He said it, it must come to pass.

Wait for it and do not get discouraged. Whenever you are in such a situation where your belief is challenged as Martha's (there is always a time like it), you have the right to be angry but there is something you must remember, He never disappoints.

It might look like He is late and sure He is never in a hurry but He is always on time. The scripture says be angry, but sin not. Always bear it in mind that God has promised never to leave or forsake you and you must learn to give Him the chance He needs, to prove Himself. Patience is a very vital tool required in your dealing with God.

The believer should therefore develop a constant attitude of patience in every situation and wait on the Lord who never fails. He remains the same and can never see you and change.

A Samaritan woman, who came to the well to get water, saw Jesus sitting by the side. She never knew Jesus, but her encounter with Him that day is a very interesting story recorded in the book of John 4. The disciples of Jesus had gone to buy food, so He was alone when this woman came there. Jesus may not have been tasty when He told her, to give Him water to drink. He may have just wanted to establish a conversation with the woman and so, He asked her for water to drink.

From this point, they had a very long and interesting conversation. Let us see, some important verses for her story as recorded in John 4:

21 Jesus saith unto her, woman believe me, the hour cometh, when ye shall neither in this mountain, nor yet at Jerusalem, worship the Father.

25 The woman saith unto him, I know that Messias cometh, which is called Christ: when he is come, he will tell us all things. 26 Jesus saith unto her, I that speak unto thee am *he*.

28 The woman then left her waterpot, and went her way into the city, and saith to the men, 29 Come, see a man, which told me all things that ever I did: is not this the Christ? 30 Then they went out of the city, and came unto him. 39 And many of the Samaritans of that city believed on him for the saying of the woman, which testified, He told me all that ever I did.

I also think that when Jesus saw this woman, knowing all things, He saw her heart and that was why He decided to established a conversation with her. The woman showed that she had an idea about a Messiah that would come. She believed in the Messiah and carried it on her mind even while she was marrying and re-marrying. She was even at the time of meeting Jesus, living with a man who was not her husband. But her belief on the Messiah that was to come was very strong.

Jesus simply said, I am He and the woman ran into her city to broadcast it and she ended up attracting so many people who believed on Him due to her sayings. She was not a pretender. She acted out of her inner most feeling and nothing could stop her.

The today's believe system, is hampered by religion and the environment. People tend not to believe in themselves, talk more of believing in another person. But it does not mean that you cannot be different. You don't have to believe in man, just believe in God and in Him alone.

God's word is clear and true. It says that God knows those that are His and it warned us to be careful, not to be deceived. So then, if you are deceived, you won't say that you were not warned. It is those who believe, that He gave power to be called the children of God. Therefore belief is a key to the heart of God.

The unbeliever has no place in the presence of God. That is why it is also written, that everything is possible for the one who believes. Whatever you asked for in prayer, believe that you have received it and it will be yours.

There is no other way to God except through Jesus Christ. Jesus, speaking in John chapter 14 verses 1-3, 6 made a very serious statement implicating Himself because He was sure of whom He is. He said the following:

1 Let not your heart be troubled: ye believe in God, believe also in me. 2 In my Father's house are many mansions: if *it were* not *so*, I would have told you. I go to prepare a place for you. 3 And if I go and prepare a place for you, I will come again, and receive you unto myself; that where I am, there ye may be also.

6 Jesus saith unto him, I am the way, the truth, and the life: no man cometh unto the Father, but by me.

There is no other religion that has the same promises, Jesus made in this John 14. When Jesus spoke those words, you were not yet born, but He had you in mind. He said let not your heart, be troubled. That is, ease yourself of all your troubles. No matter how large the troubles may look in your hands, hand them over to Him by believing in God and also in Him.

Do not count on man, count only on Him and His Father and He will make every provision available for you. Do not be afraid to believe. He added that if it were not so, He would have told you. He said it plainly, I am the way. This means that the mountains are not the way, either are seas, the rivers or the streams and everything in them. The thick forests and the rocks are also not the way or the blood of any other sacrifice. Jesus did it all!

The word of God is very clear on who your belief should be on. The world and everything in it shall definitely pass away. You are here in the world as a pilgrimage. So long as you are a true believer in Jesus Christ, you are not of the world. All that is happening in the world today is a sign that the Son of God shall return at the appointed time. He said that He did not know the time, but only the Father knows it. He added as written in Matthew 24, saying therefore be ready.

For in such an hour as you think not, the Son of man shall come. The faithful and wise servant is the one the Lord shall find doing what He had commanded. He shall make him ruler over all His goods. But and if the servant becomes evil and say in his heart, my lord delays his coming and he begin to smite his fellow servants and to eat and drink with the drunkard, the lord of that servant shall come in a day when he did not expect Him and in an hour that he is not aware of. And shall cut him asunder and appoint him his portion with the hypocrites: there shall be weeping and gnashing of teeth.

It is written, that the commandment of God is that you should believe in the name of His son Jesus Christ and love one another as He gave us commandment. Be ready and wait patiently on the Almighty God. He that will come must surely come. Also be wise and keep on doing the Lord's biddings. Do not say that He has delayed to come and begin to withdraw and follow the unbelievers to do what they do. Always reject the voice of men, it never agrees with the voice of God.

CHAPTER FOUR: Faithful Woman

NOW FAITH IS THE SUBSTANCE OF THINGS HOPED FOR, THE EVIDENCE OF THINGS NOT SEEN. FOR BY IT THE ELDERS OBTAINED A GOOD REPORT. THROUGH FAITH WE UNDERSTAND THAT THE WORLDS WERE FRAMED BY THE WORD OF GOD, SO THAT THINGS WHICH ARE SEEN WERE NOT MADE OF THINGS WHICH DO APPEAR, BUT WITHOUT FAITH *IT IS* IMPOSSIBLE TO PLEASE *HIM.* FOR HE THAT COMETH TO GOD MUST BELIEVE THAT HE IS, AND *THAT* HE IS A REWARDER OF THEM THAT DILIGENTLY SEEK HIM.

My understanding from the first part of the scripture above found in the book of Hebrews 11; is that faith is a substance just as water is a substance. For instance, when the weather changes and the sky becomes cloudy, like events changes negatively in our lives and things becomes cloudy, there is always fear of the unknown. This is where faith is required. You do not know where the circumstance is going to take you, but you suddenly develop confidence and begin to hope in God as your source. Whenever this is the case, there is always a testimony.

In the case of the weather, when there is a change in the sky and it becomes cloudy, it is always believed that there will be rain. You then begin to make arrangement in expectation of the rain. You set your water drums in place so that when it eventually comes, you can get water which is the substance you need to sustain yourself.

You do not expect a storm that would destroy properties, so you are not afraid. You simply hope or believe that a circumstance shall not consume you even when you do not know how it is going to be, you are not afraid. Therefore, the evidence of your hope which you did not see but believed is faith.

For instance, a woman says to her son, see the weather and she instructs him to move fast before the rain comes down. The son begins to run as fast as he could because his mother has warned about a coming rain. They have not seen the rain, but the hope that it is coming. It might not rain at that moment they had expected it, but the fact is that the weather condition triggered an expectation for a coming rain and by this expectation they are able to pack the corn spread outside and gather the cloths left to dry under the sun.

The faith you have must be tried and this is why Peter wrote the following in the book of 1 Peter chapter 1; "6 Wherein ye greatly rejoice, though now for a season, if need be, ye are in heaviness through manifold temptations: 7 That the trial of your faith, being much more precious than of gold that perisheth, though it be tried with fire, might be found unto praise and honour and glory at the appearing of Jesus Christ: 8 Whom having not seen, ye love; in whom, though now ye see him not, yet believing, ye rejoice with joy unspeakable and full of glory: 9 Receiving the end of your faith, even the salvation of your souls".

Jesus in Mark chapter 11 verses 22 said, "Have faith in God". This faith is an ingredient required in the lives of every Christian. But how do you get to have it?

The Bible has this to say in Romans chapter 10 verses 17: "So then faith cometh by hearing and hearing by the word of God". It comes by hearing and not just hearing anything, but hearing the word of God.

You need to hear and hear the word of God, for faith to develop in you. It is mentioned in the word of God as one of the fruit of the Spirit. The woman with the issue of blood, who Jesus told that her faith had made her whole, heard that Jesus was passing before she went to touch His garment. See Mark chapter 5 verses 27:

"When she had heard of Jesus, came in the press behind, and touched his garment". When she touched His Him and was made well, Jesus said to her, "Daughter, thy faith hath made thee whole; go in peace, and be whole of thy plague".

She would not have heard, if she was not listening. First she was desirous of hearing and when she listened to the story that was going around everywhere about the son of God, this story influenced her. She picked it and set herself in the position where she would see and touch Jesus.

It is recorded that she had suffered many things of many physicians and even though she had spent all that she had, she grew worse. One may ask, how then did she grow faith so quick? The answer is that she had heard of Jesus over time and while she heard of how He healed a lot of other people, her faith in Him grew.

The second part of the Bible verses found in the box at the beginning of this chapter, which is also a record from the same book of Hebrews chapter 11 but it is in verse 6 and says, "Without faith it is impossible to please God". God Himself confirmed this statement by His word in Deuteronomy chapter 32 verses 20, shown here below:

20 And he said I will hide my face from them, I will see what their end *shall be*: for they *are* a very froward generation, children in whom *is* no faith.

God is definitely angry with faithlessness. He wants you to have faith in Him and in His word. Jesus said in His word, that if you have faith as small as a mustard seed, you can move mountains. You can agree with me, that the mustard seed is too little in size, but Jesus used it to give example as to the size of faith that is expected from a child of God.

Let me make a reference once more to the widow of Zarephath. It was the faith of this woman that prompted her to give to Prophet Elijah. Even after she told Elijah about her plan to eat her last meal with her son and die, she went ahead to do what he requested her to do. She heard the word of God which strengthened her faith. See how the scripture recorded the words that Elijah spoke to her in the book of 2 kings chapter 17:

13 And Elijah said unto her, Fear not; go *and* do as thou hast said: but make me thereof a little cake first, and bring *it* unto me, and after make for thee and for thy son. 14 For thus saith the LORD God of Israel, the barrel of meal shall not waste, neither shall the cruse of oil fail, until the day *that* the LORD sendeth rain upon the earth.

Here again is the Shunammite woman. The first time you read about her in this book, it had to do with her giving. Now I want to talk about her faith. Remember that Elisha prayed for her to be pregnant and it was so. The Bible recorded that she gave birth to a baby boy. But it happened at that time, that the baby died and the woman took a radical action. She said nothing to her husband about what had happened. She laid the child on a bed inside a room and went to meet the man of God.

So she came to the man of God at Mount Carmel. And as she was coming, the man of God saw her from afar off. He said to Gehazi his servant, look, there *is* that Shunammite. Please run now to meet her and ask her, Is it well with thee? Is it well with thy husband? Is *it* well with the child? The servant of Elisha ran as he was instructed and when he asked her all the questions, she answered, It is well.

What exactly is well in this circumstance? Was it well that a woman had an only child and the child was dead? The only ground someone can stand on to make such statement in such circumstance is the ground of faith. Understand me. It's not ordinary faith, its faith coated with hard stones. She had hope that the dead child will come back to life and the evidence was in her statement, it is well. When this kind of faith is put on a scale against any weight, it always weighs higher.

Many times, you are faced with situations that cannot be compared to the death of an only child and you call God names, making Him a liar. You quickly forget the last thing He did in your favor because you want more. This woman held on to her faith and God saw it and loved her. Her dead child cannot remain dead in that circumstance. God gave him back to her.

Naomi was an interesting woman. She was the mother in-law of Ruth who was Moabites, but followed Naomi to Bethlehem. I think what happened, was that Naomi told Ruth a lot of stories about the God of Israel and these stories she heard helped to build her faith in God.

This faith grew to the point where Ruth had believed, that she must be favored no matter how sad things looked. So she decided to go with her mother in-law who could not understand the young woman because she didn't realize that the words she released when she told her beautiful stories about the goodness of God, stuck with her.

Once you keep hearing the word of God you can never know where faith will meet up with you. One important thing is to build on the word and have it with you wherever you go. On one occasion after they had both returned to Bethlehem, Ruth said to her mother in-law, "Let me go to the field and glean ears of corn". This lady just got into a town where she was not born nor did she grow up there, so she knew no one or anywhere. Where did she think, she was going to glean the corn?

I will maintain, that her faith was built around the stories her mother in-law told her. Naomi had always told her that her people were good people, who cared for each other and strangers. She told her that the God of Israel always favored anyone who does well and so Ruth went out in full hope of being favored.

As it was, it is recorded that she found favor even beyond her own imagination. She was over whelmed by Boaz gesture to her. In Ruth chapter 2 verses 8-9, she met Boaz who told her, not to glean in any other field nor go from his. He advised her, to stay with his maidens and keep her eyes on the field that they reap, going after them. He assured her, that he had charged the young men not to touch her and that if she thirsts, she should go to the vessels, to drink of that which the young men have drawn.

That was what the faith of Ruth, brought to her. It was this Boaz, that married her and they became the parents of

Obed who was the father of Jesse, the father of David the king of Israel. Do you see how faith pays off? As I said here, the stories she heard played a great part in putting all this in place. Remember faith comes by hearing and hearing by the word of God. You can never grow in faith unless you grow in hearing the word of God.

Moses the man of God married the daughter of Jethro, the priest of Midian. The name of his wife was Zipporah and this woman knew nothing about the God of Israel except the stories she was told by her husband and probably her father. At one time, something interesting happened.

God attempted to take Moses' life but Zipporah took a sharp stone and cut off the foreskin of her son which she cast at his feet and said, surely you a bloody husband to me. At this, God let Moses go. She said, you are a bloody husband, because of the circumcision.

Zipporah was able to save her husband by the blood of circumcision. Who told her about that? Her husband, I guess. He shared the word of God with his wife telling her about the covenant God made with Abraham and as soon as she heard it, she stored it. Now in the circumstance they found themselves, she decided to make use of what she heard and it worked.

Again it was the stories this woman heard, that helped her to develop the faith that saved her husband's life. Remember that she was a Midianite just like Ruth so if she had not heard the word through the stories she had heard, she would have lost her husband.

By simply sharing stories, you can pass on useful information to a relative or friends and this information might come up at a later time to be the source of help for you and those who heard you. You can never know the extent a little meaningful story can go in building a strong faith.

Jesus did not tell all stories He told His disciples, because He was a story teller. No, He told so many stories in order to build up the people around Him. He knew what they needed to grow and He kept on feeding them.

Rahab was a harlot recorded in the book of Joshua chapter. Her story has it that she took in the spies sent to her country by Joshua and hid them from the soldiers who were sent by the king to search for them in her house. She had gone to the spies and had a discussion with them before letting them go. She told them plainly, what she had heard about their people and their God. Obviously, it was what she heard that gave her the confidence to do what she did.

She told the story of what she heard about the God of Israel in Joshua chapter 2. She said that they had heard how the Lord dried up the water of the Red sea for the Israelites, when they came out of Egypt and what they did to the two kings of the Amorites, that were on the other side of Jordan, Sihon and Og, whom the children of Israel utterly destroyed. And as soon as she and her people heard these things, their hearts melted.

All of them lost courage, including all the men of the land because of the Israelites. From the stories they heard, they concluded, that the Lord and God of the children of Israel, is God in heaven above and in earth beneath and they were troubled.

Someone else who heard the same stories; may have become afraid and ran, but Rahab heard it and it helped to build her faith. By this therefore, God saw her and noted how ready she was to be used by Him. This was why, God decided to use her at that time. What she heard was the word of God. A story of what God had done and is doing for His people Israel.

That was enough to build the faith of a harlot to the point of saving the spies in order to save herself and her entire family. She actually took a risk that would have taken her own life, but at that time, she did not see what she did as a risk. She instead saw safety for her entire family. That is unreserved faith at work.

In the book of Hebrews chapter 11: 31, the scripture says; by faith, the harlot Rahab perished not with them that believed not, when she had received the spies with peace.

She heard, believed and faith grew in her. The Bible says, he who has ear, hear what the Spirit is saying. Since the whole word of God was written by the inspiration of the Holy Spirit, one has no option than to set his or her heart on what is written. Forget whatever anyone might have to say and hold on to what the word of God says.

Read the word constantly and continuously and your faith will increase beyond measure. If you know what you want and you search the word of God, you must see a similar case. It is now left for you, to liken your case to what is written and claim the victory that God provided in His word.

In order to scare her away, Jesus spoke careless words to the woman of Canaan who met Him for the healing of her daughter. But this woman refused to give up. I mentioned her as a praying woman in the other chapter and now she is coming up again as a faithful woman. She had heard about the healing power of Jesus and also heard His word going through her region and these helped to build her faith in Him.

At the end of it all, Jesus made this powerful statement to her, "O woman, great is thy faith: be it unto thee even as thou wilt. And her daughter was made whole from that very hour".

You can agree with me, that this woman went to war and as she came to the war front, bullets were coming towards her radically. Instead of being discouraged, she lay low and kept moving forward because she knew that even though the front was hot, the end would be in her favor. She knew that going back was not the right way. It was better she fought once and win the enemy than to run back and never be able to stand before him (enemy), forever. She made the better choice and stood her ground. It was not easy, but you and I know that nothing good comes easy.

Another woman that I will like to bring into this chapter is the mother of Samson. Her story came up in the book of Judges 13. This woman was reported as barren and the angel of God visited her and gave her a message. The message brought by the angel that came to her, was that she will conceive and bear a son. Being alone on the day she received that message, she went home and told her husband what had happened while she was alone.

Now the Bible has it, that her husband Manoah wanted to see the man (angel), himself so he prayed to God asking Him to send him back to them. In answer to that prayer, the angel visited this woman again and again her husband was not with her. So she had to run, to go and invite her husband, telling him that he (angel) had come. As at this time, Manoah did not know that their visitor was an angel of God.

He asked him some questions and offered to give him something to eat. The Bible says that the man asked them to forget about him and make a burnt offering to God. They made quick and brought what they had, but something strange happened as soon as they offered the burnt offering.

Manoah took a kid with a meat offering and offered it upon a rock to the Lord and the angel did wonderously as Manoah and his wife looked on. When the flame went up toward heaven from off the altar, the angel of the Lord ascended in the flame of the altar while Manoah and his wife looked on it and they fell on their faces to the ground.

The angel of the Lord disappeared before Manoah and his wife. It was then, that Manoah knew that he was an angel of the Lord. He said to his wife, we shall surely die, because we have seen God. But his wife told him, that if the Lord was pleased to kill them, He would not have received the burnt and a meat offering from them and He would not have shown them all the things that they saw nor told them the things they were told at that time.

Can you see the faith of this woman? While her husband was afraid of the consequences of seeing an angel of God, his wife reasoned differently. It is obvious that she knew more about God than her husband. I guess that was because, she was considered barren. She must have been going closer to God through her prayers and heard His word more often than her husband did.

She may have also slept in the temple severally and relied on stories of the wonders of the God of Israel which as she had heard, grew her faith in God. She believed that God cannot kill her and her husband. She noted that the Lord accepted their burnt offering, showed and told them things He would not have told the people He was angry with. She was sure, that what happened, would not lead to disaster and her assurance was based on her faith in God. Where do you base your assurance?

Permit me to talk about Esther here. I want to add her because I think there is something to learn from how her faith grew. Someone might ask, if she was faithful and my answer to it will be that I think so. When her uncle approached her to do something in order to save her people, she was fearful and faithless. But as her uncle continued to pressure, speak and remind her of whom God is, her faith was rekindled. Someone like Esther needed someone like Mordecai to restart her faith.

If there was no Mordecai to hear the word of God from, there would have been no faith in Esther. She gave all the excuses that were available to her, but her uncle insisted. He did not let her rest. Then suddenly, something woke in her. She realized who she was. She remembered that she was a daughter of Zion and that God the creator of heaven and earth was her Father.

Fasting, was a tradition she was accustomed to from the time she was a little girl. So she simply went back to it and the spark came right back. That was how she made a mark on the wall of fame as a woman loved and used by God in working for His people.

By the third day of the fasting, she was filled with faith and went to meet the king against all odds. Even after the king had made her an offer, she scheduled an appointment so that Haman who was the traitor of her people will be invited to a banquet. The king was fast to bring Haman and again asked Esther to state her request which he was ready to do for her. But her faith had grown too strong to be punctured half way. She instead, scheduled another appointment for the king and Haman to eat her banquet the second time.

At this point, her faith had become unstoppable. The first response of the king, on the first day she appeared before him made Esther scream. She thought to herself, this God is wonderful and then she decided to go all the way.

She was going to throw all her cards on the table. It was her faith against the odds. She did not become afraid that the king might change his mind, she was trusting in the Lord who had begun the good work for her and she believed that He shall see it to a successful completion. Her testimony is the essence of the book of Esther.

Again, Mary the mother of Jesus will also come in here because she was a faithful woman. From the way she took the words of the angel that visited her, you can agree with me that she had been hearing and storing the word of God in her heart until her faith was full. Imagine a young woman who was bestowed to a man, accepting such an assignment.

But looking at her prayers in the book of Luke chapter 1 from verses 46-55, you will see that she was full of the word of God and God must have said I have found her; she is the one.

Help me to read this her prayer copied from the bible and enclosed here as follows:

46 And Mary said, my soul doth magnify the Lord, 47 And my spirit hath rejoiced in God my Saviour. 48 For he hath regarded the low estate of his handmaiden: for, behold, from henceforth all generations shall call me blessed. 49 For he that is mighty hath done to me great things; and holy *is* his name. 50 And his mercy *is* on them that fear him from generation to generation.

51 He hath showed strength with his arm; he hath scattered the proud in the imagination of their hearts. 52 He hath put down the mighty from *their* seats, and exalted them of low degree. 53 He hath filled the hungry with good things; and the rich he hath sent empty away. 54 He hath holpen his servant Israel, in remembrance of *his* mercy; 55 As he spake to our fathers, to Abraham, and to his seed for ever.

You can see from the above reference, that Mary confirmed her hungry which God filled. She also testified that she was of low degree. That is the kind of person God is looking for. He is looking for those who are hoping on Him alone, those who have no other alternative but depends on Him completely. God wants you to build your faith on what you have heard Him say and accept it as the only thing that is available.

The Lord our God is always searching your heart in order to see the level of your faith. It is by faith that you are saved. When your heart is filled with faith, it is easier to deal with God because He is also faithful and uses the content of the faith in your life to deal with you.

See what the scripture says in Galatians chapter three:

6 Even as Abraham believed God, and it was accounted to him for righteousness. 7 Know ye therefore that they which are of faith, the same are the children of Abraham. 8 And the scripture, foreseeing that God would justify the heathen through faith, preached before the gospel unto Abraham, saying, in thee shall all nations be blessed. 9 So then they which be of faith are blessed with faithful Abraham.

Can you remember that harlot named Rahab in the book of Joshua? This woman did not see Jesus or heard about Him, but you child of God have heard about Jesus and read His word. You are therefore different from Rahab. The Bible says something in Hebrews chapter 10, which I brought in here for you to see and read. It says;

19 Having therefore, brethren, boldness to enter into the holiest by the blood of Jesus, 20 By a new and living way, which he hath consecrated for us, through the veil, that is to say, his flesh; 21 And having an high priest over the house of God; 22 Let us draw near with a true heart in full assurance of faith, having our hearts sprinkled from an evil conscience, and our bodies washed with pure water.

23 Let us hold fast the profession of our faith without wavering; (for he is faithful that promised;) 24 And let us consider one another to provoke unto love and to good works: 25 Not forsaking the assembling of ourselves together, as the manner of some is; but exhorting one another: and so much the more, as ye see the day approaching.

The difference is clear. You have received boldness to enter into the holiest through the blood of Jesus, so you must draw near with a true heart in full assurance of faith. Hold on the profession of your faith without wavering. God has made a promise and He is faithful to fulfill His word.

The Bible asked a question and answered it as follows; "For what if some did not believe? Shall their unbelief make the faith of God without effect? God forbid: yea, let God be true, but every man a liar; as it is written, That thou mightest be justified in thy sayings, and mightest overcome when thou art judged".

CHAPTER FIVE: Loving Woman

> BELOVED, LET US LOVE ONE ANOTHER: FOR LOVE IS OF GOD; AND EVERY ONE THAT LOVETH IS BORN OF GOD, AND KNOWETH GOD. HE THAT LOVETH NOT KNOWETH NOT GOD; FOR GOD IS LOVE.
>
> HEREIN IS LOVE, NOT THAT WE LOVED GOD, BUT THAT HE LOVED US, AND SENT HIS SON *TO BE* THE PROPITIATION FOR OUR SINS. BELOVED, IF GOD SO LOVED US, WE OUGHT ALSO TO LOVE ONE ANOTHER. NO MAN HATH SEEN GOD AT ANY TIME. IF WE LOVE ONE ANOTHER, GOD DWELLETH IN US, AND HIS LOVE IS PERFECTED IN US.

God is love and to show that you are a child of God, you ought to continue to love. The word of God confirms that if you do not love, you do not know God.

Love is not that you love God. No. Love is that He loves you and His Son died for you on the cross of Calvary. No one has seen God at any time, but when you love, God will make your heart His abode and dwell with you. Therefore, the woman God loves is the woman who has a heart of love. What I mean here, is not the carnal kind of love which is of the flesh. I am talking about the agape love which is purely unconditional and sacrificial. It comes with no strings attached.

The word of God says that God so loved the world that He gave His only Son to die for mankind. This act of God alone, is an evidence that love is powerful. See what Paul wrote in Romans chapter 5: 7, For scarcely for a righteous man will one die: yet peradventure for a good man some would even dare to die. 8 But God commendeth his love toward us, in that, while we were yet sinners, Christ died for us.

Jesus taught His disciples how love should be in John chapter 14. He told them, that the one who hears His commandments and keep them, loves Him and he that loves Him shall be loved by His Father and Himself and the two of them (Father and Son), will manifest themselves to him.

Then Judas, not Iscariot asked Him, Lord, how is it that you will manifest yourself to us and not to the world? He answered and said to him, if a man loves me, he will keep my words and my Father will love him and we will come to him to make our dwelling with him. He that does not love me; will not keep my sayings and the word which you hear are not mine, but the Father's which sent me.

He continued in the next chapter of John, chapter 15 to teach them further, reminding them of the things he had said. He told them that He loved them as the Father had loved Him and advised them to continue in His love. He again reminded them, that if they keep His commandments, they shall abide in His love; just as He kept His Father's commandments and abide in His love.

He added that He spoke to them, so that His joy might remain in them and that their joy might be full. In conclusion, He said, "This is my commandment, that you love one another, as I have loved you". There's no greater love than that a man laid down His life for His friends.

As Jesus prayed for His disciples, He said Father, I will that they also, whom You have given me, be with me where I am; that they may behold my glory, which You have given me: for You loved me before the foundation of the world. He continued and said, "O righteous Father, the world has not known You but I have known You and these have known that You sent me. I have declared to them Your name and will declare it: that the love wherewith You have loved me may be in them and I in them".

Agape love is the kind of love which God has for you, child of God. His love towards you is unconditional and sacrificial. He has spread this love through the Holy Spirit on those who believe and have faith in Him. The love of God makes an ordinary person to become extra-ordinary.

There is this story in the book of 1 kings chapter 3. The story has it, that two harlots had delivered babies and at night the baby of one died. When they woke up in the morning of the next day, there was a very big struggle over the ownership of the living child. One said that the living baby belonged to her and the other said same. This continued until their matter was reported to the king for him to determine, the case.

At that time, Solomon the son of David was the king of Israel and God had given him wisdom beyond man's understanding. So the king took a decision, to split the living child into two so that each one of the women could have one part. But the woman whose, the living child belonged to, told the king to give it to the other woman and not to slay it.

The other woman however agreed that the child should be spitted so that neither she nor the other woman should have it. The true mother of the living child could not withstand her child being cut with a knife in her presence, but the imposter insisted that it should be done as the king suggested.

Love had a chance to speak in this incident. No loving mother can hold back herself while her baby is being killed in cold blood. No matter what might be the case, a true mother must always prefer to give herself in an exchange for her child. It took her nine months to carry the pregnancy and deliver that child therefore whoever, is going to take the child from her must have to kill her first before taking the fruit of her suffering.

Paul's writing on love in the book of 1 Corinthians 13; is too powerful and teaches a lot of things about the God's kind of love. In trying to define and explain love, he said that though he had the gift of prophecy, and understood all mysteries, and all knowledge; and though he had all faith, so that he could remove mountains, and have not love, he is nothing.

He added that though he bestowed all his goods to feed the poor, and though he gave his body to be burned, and have not love, it profits him nothing. He said that love suffers long, and is kind; love envieth not; love vaunteth not itself, is not puffed up, does not behave itself unseemly, seeks not her own, is not easily provoked, thinks no evil; rejoices not in iniquity, but rejoices in the truth; bears all things, believes all things, hopes all things and endures all things.

He continued and said that love never fails but whether there are prophecies, they shall fail, whether there are tongues, they shall cease and whether there is knowledge, it shall vanish away. For we, know in part and we prophesy in part. But when, that which is perfect comes then that which is in part shall be done away with.

112

He ended by saying, "When I was a child, I spoke like a child, I understood like a child, I thought like a child: but when I became a man, I put away childish things. For now we see through a glass, darkly; but then face to face: now I know in part; but then shall I know even as also I am known. And now abideth faith, hope, love, these three; but the greatest of these is love".

Paul's writing shows, that nothing can be compared to this God's kind of love. It is patient, it is kind, it does not envy, and it does not boast, it is not proud, it does not dishonor others, it is not self seeking, it is not easily angered and it keeps no record of wrongs. It does not delight in evil, but rejoices with the truth. It always protects, always trusts, always hopes and always perseveres.

The God's kind of love, never fails. Can you tell me what you can compare to it? You may have gifts, understand mysteries and all knowledge; have faith that can move mountains but without this love, heaven considers you as nothing.

Paul also wrote in Romans 12, to teach us how this God's kind of love should be. He said that it should be without dissimulation and avoid what is evil, holding on to what is good. We should be kindly affectionate to each other with brotherly love; in honour preferring one another; not slothful in business; fervent in spirit; serving the Lord; rejoicing in hope; patient in tribulation; continuing instant in prayer; distributing to the necessity of saints; given to hospitality. Bless them that persecute you: bless and do not curse. Rejoice with them that rejoice and weep with them that weep.

He advised that we should be, of the same mind towards each other, not minding high things, but condescend to men of low estate. When we are in love, we should not be wise in our own eyes and pay evil for evil. Instead, we should provide things honest in the sight of all men. If it is possible, as much as it depends on you, live at peace with all men.

He continued and said, dearly beloved; do not avenge by yourselves, but rather give way to wrath: for it is written, Vengeance is mine; I will repay, said the Lord. Therefore if your enemy hunger, feed him; if he thirst, give him drink: for by doing so, you shall heap coals of fire on his head. Do not be overcome with evil, but overcome evil with good.

In Ephesians chapter one, this same Paul had this to say from verses 3 to 4; 3 Blessed be the God and Father of our Lord Jesus Christ, who hath blessed us with all spiritual blessings in heavenly places in Christ: 4 According as he hath chosen us in him before the foundation of the world, that we should be holy and without blame before him in love:

Men may be deceived, but heaven can never be deceived. The contents of this kind of love cannot be hidden. It is not something you can say, that you left at home or that you are not in the mood for because the God's kind of love is always built in to match. Once you see a carrier of this kind of love, they are always too obvious and cannot hide. If you have it or if you don't have it, it is also always open to all. You may pretend with every other thing and deceive people, but pretending to have this God's kind love is out of the way.

One day, Jesus went to the house of a Pharisees who had invited him to come and eat with him and his friends, in his house. As Jesus was seated in the house, something happened that made those with him to murmur. A woman came in there and did what no one thought was possible.

This woman was known in the city to be a sinner and so the people were wondering why Jesus did not know who she was and stopped her from coming to touch Him. The people began to say, that if Jesus was who He said He was; He should have stopped the woman.

But Jesus did not see it the way they saw it. What He saw, was the heart of this woman which was filled with love for Him. Knowing also the hearts of the people around Him, Jesus did a remarkable thing noted in Luke chapter 7, from verses 44 to 48 as follows:

44 And he turned to the woman, and said unto Simon, Seest thou this woman? I entered into thine house, thou gavest me no water for my feet: but she hath washed my feet with tears, and wiped *them* with the hairs of her head. 45 Thou gavest me no kiss: but this woman since the time I came in hath not ceased to kiss my feet.

46 My head with oil thou didst not anoint: but this woman hath anointed my feet with ointment. 47 Wherefore I say unto thee, her sins, which are many, are forgiven; for she loved much: but to whom little is forgiven, the same loveth little. 48 And he said unto her, Thy sins are forgiven.

The love in the heart of this woman helped her to approach Jesus like no one else did and her many sins were forgiven her. It was not pretence. All she did, she did from the innermost part of her heart. She did not do it to be noticed, she did it because there was something burning inside her.

The record does not say that she made any statement, talking with her mouth. Her actions said all that she needed to say. As she was washing his feet with her tears and wiping them with her hair, the action spoke. Nothing could contend with this kind of love. Not even the presence of the men there could stop her or the way that they looked at her. She knew who she was, but she must have thought to herself, that it was in the past. Jesus said that she had loved more.

The woman that did all this was Mary Magdalene. You read about her in the previous chapter of this book because she was phenomenal in the acts of the women of the Bible. She followed Jesus from the time she met Him, to the time of His death and resurrection. She was the first person that saw Jesus after He resurrected.

She had gone to call the disciples who ran to the grave where Jesus was buried and after they left, she stood there and wept because the body of Jesus was missing. Then Jesus suddenly stood behind her and asked her why she was weeping and who she was looking for. She, supposing Him to be the gardener saith to him, Sir, if you took Him, tell me where you have laid him and I will take him away. Jesus called her, "Mary". She turned and said to him, Rabboni; which is to say, Master.

Why didn't this woman go home with the others? I guess you know the answer. She loved the Lord and she needed answer to what had happened to His body. So she stayed there wondering and hoping to get an answer. The angels who were at the grave saw her weeping and asked her why she wept. Her answer to them was that some people had taken the body of the Lord and she knew not where they had laid Him.

This happened before she heard a sound and turned herself to see Jesus standing there. Not knowing that it was Jesus, He also asked her why she wept and who she was looking for. She said to Him, Sir if you have taken Him, tell me where you laid Him and I will take Him away.

It was at this point, that Jesus called out her name and she responded by calling Him Master.

I am not sure, that I can demonstrate this scene through writing. Let me try to describe it as much as I can. Just imagine how Jesus must have called her name stretching it and how she may have responded to Him with an exclamation in her voice. Since she just suddenly realized that it was Jesus, there will be excitement mixed with fear in her voice. She may have felt like running back, but why run when what you were looking for was there before you.

You see, true love is magical. It defeats fear and always looks stupid because no one can ever describe it as it is. A love with a reason is a love that is meant to fail. Imagine the love that God bestowed on you, that you are called a child of God. Do you really deserve it? If put on a scale, what do you think, you will weigh before God? But God neglected your imperfection and continued to love you even when you have proved so difficult to be loved.

Do you know that after Adam and Eve did what they did in the Garden of Eden, God still clothed them? This is how God wants you to love; unconditionally and sacrificial.

See enclosed, the advice Jesus gave to His followers in the Matthew chapter 5 from verses 43-48:

43 Ye have heard that it hath been said thou shalt love thy neighbour, and hate thine enemy. 44 But I say unto you, Love your enemies, bless them that curse you, do good to them that hate you, and pray for them which despitefully use you, and persecute you; 45 That ye may be the children of your Father which is in heaven: for he maketh his sun to rise on the evil and on the good, and sendeth rain on the just and on the unjust. 46 For if ye love them which love you, what reward have ye? Do not even the publicans the same? 47 And if ye salute your brethren only, what do ye more than others? Do not even the publicans so? 48 Be ye therefore perfect, even as your Father which is in heaven is perfect.

I know you have heard people say that no one is perfect, but Jesus said you should be perfect. If He said, that you should be perfect, it means that you can be perfect and there is perfection in love. According to John in the book of 1 John chapter 4, perfect love brings about boldness. When you love as the Father of all creation does, you can come boldly on the Day of Judgment without any fear because perfect love cast out fear.

It is written, that you should love your enemies and bless them that curse you. Do good to them that hate you, pray for them that despitefully use you and persecute you so that you may be the children of your Father in heaven. Your Father in heaven makes His sun to rise on the evil and the good. He sends rain on the just and the unjust. He is God you may say, but He also made you to be like Him. Therefore you can do what He does. Jesus loved Judas who was His enemy and was with him until he betrayed Him.

At the time Jesus was with Judas, He (Jesus); did something. He told Judas that he was the betrayer. This simply put means, that you must face that your enemy and tell him/her what you know. The enemy might deny, but your boldness will be a shock to such person(s). Bless your enemy by telling him/her face to face, that even though he/she wishes you bad, you wish him/her well. Though you know the enemy hates you, do well to them. Send gifts to them; ask how they are doing and even pay them unscheduled visits.

Praying for your enemy is very simple because you know, that you are not like them. When you pray therefore, you simply go to God with the details of what the enemy is doing or has done to you. Then tell God to put them on His list and consider them. Make a request on God, ask Him to weigh the two sides accordingly, on His scale and see how to vindicate you. Let God Himself, be the one to judge the case. We read in His words, that vengeance belongs to Him.

If you do not put your side in order and pray for your enemy to die, the enemy will keep living and this will bring discouragement to you. But when you have taken care of your side by following the orders of Jesus and pray for God to arise in the case between you and the enemy, He will arise with the right judgment. He never forsakes the righteous. The prayer of the righteous is always like, a sweet smelling incense to God.

You can be taught to love, just as you can be taught, to give, pray and have faith. This is what God has been doing with mankind from creation. He has been trying to teach you and I, to love the way He loves us. Even though man has been difficult to teach, He has continued to bring teachers from amongst men from generation to generation, to teach His people according to His will for us.

Reading through the Bible, you will agree with me that almost all the men God used, practiced and taught love. The Apostle Peter in 1 Peter 3; 1-2, advised wives to be subjection to their own husbands so that if any obey not the word, they also may without the word be won by the conversation of the wives; as they see their chaste conversation coupled with fear.

Being in subjection to a husband requires the God kind of love. If a woman does not have this love in her heart, she cannot be submissive. The list of what God's kind of love does, shows that it is required in marriage and in the family because it will play a vital role in harmonizing both sides.

Where God's love is lacking in any marriage, conversation between husband and wife is always altered. Therefore it is of utmost importance, that the woman keeps watching and guarding her heart. A heart that stays in God's love, will always overcome the challenges of everyday life.

Also in his letter to the Ephesians, Paul gave directives to the wives to be subject to their husbands as the church is subject to Christ. He also instructed the Corinthians in chapter 16: 14 of his 1st letter to them, to do all things in love. He had understood that if the love of God is implanted in them, they will succeed in their service to Him (God). In the same manner, he prayed for the Thessalonians in 2 Thessalonians chapter 3 verses 5, asking the Lord to direct their hearts into His love.

Titus under the leadership of Paul the Apostle; learnt the importance of this God's kind of love. Paul in writing to him, tried to teach him to build love into the hearts of the people he taught. He also spoke to the women in particular, directly. In this writing recorded in the book of Titus 3, Paul gave instructions to these women on how they can be of help to each other through holiness, behaviors and teaching.

Reading through verses 3-5, you will see what he said to the aged women. I brought the record of his writing in here for you to read the details as follow;

3 The aged women likewise, that they be in behaviour as becometh holiness, not false accusers, not given to much wine, teachers of good things; 4 That they may teach the young women to be sober, to love their husbands, to love their children, 5 To be discreet, chaste, keepers at home, good, obedient to their own husbands, that the word of God be not blasphemed.

The aged women were directed to show in themselves; behaviors of holiness and become teachers of good things. It is remarked that it is only by so doing, that they can teach the young women to be sober and love their husbands and children. By this therefore, you can understand that teaching goes beyond the use of words. It includes actions. Others may just have to look at the good behavior or character you exhibit and learn to become like you.

You know that most times, people talk more on doing good and being good but do less of it in practice. This brings a disconnection between the teacher and the learner and there can never be an understanding between the two unless the learner decides to pretend, but as I said before, there can be no pretence in the God's kind of love. This is why it is very important, that the teacher must be a symbol of what is taught for the learner to have a better understanding.

Something remarkable happened in Exodus chapter 2. This chapter of the Bible tells the story of the birth of Moses the servant of God. Moses was born at a very critical time. At the time of his birth, children his age were being killed, but his mother secured him for a reason she did not understand as at that time. Moses mother loved him and would not allow anything to happen to him. The Bible details of this story, is shown below from verses one to ten:

1 And there went a man of the house of Levi, and took *to* wife a daughter of Levi. 2 And the woman conceived, and bares a son: and when she saw him that he *was a* goodly child, she hid him three months. 3 And when she could not longer hide him, she took for him an ark of bulrushes, and daubed it with slime and with pitch, and put the child therein; and she laid *it* in the flags by the river's brink. 4 And his sister stood afar off, to wit what would be done to him.

5 And the daughter of Pharaoh came down to wash herself at the river; and her maidens walked along by the river's

side; and when she saw the ark among the flags, she sent her maid to fetch it. 6 And when she had opened *it*, she saw the child: and, behold, the babe wept. And she had compassion on him, and said, this is one of the Hebrews' children. 7 Then said his sister to Pharaoh's daughter, Shall I go and call to thee a nurse of the Hebrew women, that she may nurse the child for thee?

8 And Pharaoh's daughter said to her, Go. And the maid went and called the child's mother. 9 And Pharaoh's daughter said unto her, take this child away and nurse it for me, and I will give thee thy wages. And the woman took the child, and nursed it. 10 And the child grew, and she brought him unto Pharaoh's daughter, and he became her son. And she called his name Moses: and she said, because I drew him out of the water.

What you can see here, is that while the mother of Moses did all she did, her daughter Miriam watched her and learnt from what she saw her do. Her mother did not tell her anything nor did she expect her to do what she did, but from the way she saw her mother show compassion on her brother, the love attracted her. Before she knew it, she played a role in saving her brother.

She learnt from her mother, just by watching her do this wonderful thing and she can always say I saw my mother do it. So what are you teaching your daughter and the other girls like her around you? What are you learning from your mother and the other women around you? In all your teaching teach love, the agape love. Likewise in all your learning, learn the agape love.

James wrote in chapter 2 of his writing, saying the following;

5 Hearken, my beloved brethren, Hath not God chosen the poor of this world rich in faith, and heirs of the kingdom which he hath promised to them that love him?

Hearken here, means listen carefully. God indeed made a promise to them that love Him, to give them the kingdom. Even though they are poor in the world, they are rich in faith and heirs of the kingdom of God. This includes you, yes you. You must therefore continue in love. Do not look back to check why you should or should not love the God's way. It is a command by God that you must obey with no excuses.

See Paul's prayer for you as recorded in Philippians chapter 1; 9 And this I pray, that your love may abound yet more and more in knowledge and in all judgment; 10 That ye may approve things that are excellent; that ye may be sincere and without offence till the day of Christ; 11 Being filled with the fruits of righteousness, which are by Jesus Christ, unto the glory and praise of God.

Thanks be to the Lord, the God Almighty!

CHAPTER SIX: Caring Woman

AND HE SHALL SET THE SHEEP ON HIS RIGHT HAND, BUT THE GOATS ON THE LEFT. THEN SHALL THE KING SAY UNTO THEM ON HIS RIGHT HAND, COME, YE BLESSED OF MY FATHER, INHERIT THE KINGDOM PREPARED FOR YOU FROM THE FOUNDATION OF THE WORLD: FOR I WAS AN HUNGERED, AND YE GAVE ME MEAT: I WAS THIRSTY, AND YE GAVE ME DRINK: I WAS A STRANGER, AND YE TOOK ME IN: NAKED, AND YE CLOTHED ME: I WAS SICK, AND YE VISITED ME: I WAS IN PRISON, AND YE CAME UNTO ME.

Women are known for care and when a woman has a heart of care, she will always touch God and God will show her love. It is in caring for others that you care for yourself.

That women are known for care does not mean that all women, cares for others outside themselves and their family. Most times, women are more focused on caring for themselves and their family members only. These types of women are selfish and ignorant of the benefits of caring for others. It is often very difficult to make the woman in this category to realize, that they are making a great mistake by looking only inward.

Though such types of women are everywhere, there are others who are always more concerned about the visitors. They look at those who are not relations and friends and take care for them before looking at themselves. The women in this category are rarely liked by close family members, friends and relations because they are always seen as not being cooperative with the home front. They are called names and kept away from being part of sharing in gatherings by those family members, friends and relations they offended by their hateful attitude.

What is hateful about someone caring for people other than family, friends and relations? I think it should be a thing of joy to have such individual everywhere. These are the people God is looking for. The selfless, caring people, who are always excited by making someone else happy, they are God's kind of people. Are you one of them? Will you like to be one of them? Do you know someone like that? Have you hated someone for being like that? If you are like that or will like to be like that or know someone like that, congratulations. If you have hated someone like that, here is a chance to change.

All the women of the Bible who showed care, excelled in their time. They overcame fear and stood out as God's people because God blessed them. See Rebekah in the book of Genesis chapter 24. This young woman came to the well to get water for her family but on seeing a stranger, who looked stranded, she showed concern and attended to him not knowing why he was there or what he had come to do. She happily cared for the man and the animals with him.

This singular show of kindness attracted Abraham's servant to her. Although he had prayed, the way Rebekah cared for him marveled him. When he explained it to her family members, I am sure they must have nodded their heads in confirmation of who she was. They would have said in their hearts, "she has always been like that".

Can you imagine how many times she had cared for someone at the well? I am sure it is uncountable and God had the record. God knew she was coming to the well at that time and He knew too, that she will care for Abraham's servant and become the wife of Isaac.

Another woman of interest is Rahab. I have shared her story in a previous chapter, but I am bringing her up again to touch her care character. From the Bible story in Joshua chapter 2, this woman was on her own doing her business as a harlot. She did not know the men that came to her place but as soon as she noticed that there was trouble, she hid them.

I wish to say, that it was in the course of the questioning she received from the soldiers who came to her place, that she discovered that the men she was hiding in her place were Israelites. She initially cared for this people who came under her roof and did what she could, to protect them without knowing who they were. Yes she made requests to them, but that was after she had cared for them.

The positive response she got for her request to be saved with her family members was as a result of how she cared for the Israeli spies. When Joshua was told about her and what she did, he gave instructions concerning her and directed the men to make sure that she and her family were saved when the Israelites went into Jericho. The Bible record confirms that she and her entire family members came out alive. Even her kindred and all she had were saved. This was the result of her caring for strangers. She was also mentioned in the generation of Jesus.

See the bible details of her rescue at the fall of Jericho in Joshua chapter six below:

20 So the people shouted when *the priests* blew with the trumpets: and it came to pass, when the people heard the sound of the trumpet, and the people shouted with a great shout, that the wall fell down flat, so that the people went up into the city, every man straight before him, and they took the city. 21 And they utterly destroyed all that *was* in the city, both man and woman, young and old, and ox, and sheep, and ass, with the edge of the sword.

22 But Joshua had said unto the two men that had spied out the country, Go into the harlot's house, and bring out thence the woman, and all that she hath, as ye sware unto

her. 23 And the young men that were spies went in, and brought out Rahab, and her father, and her mother, and her brethren, and all that she had; and they brought out all her kindred, and left them without the camp of Israel.

Ruth the Moabite cared for Naomi her mother in-law. Looking at the events that followed her returning with her to Bethlehem, you will see that the true reason why she went with her was to take care of her. Once they were there, Ruth immediately began to do what she came to do.

She went out to hunt for food. She had looked at Naomi at that point when she was telling her to return to her people and wondered who would take care of this old woman. Do you think, she didn't need to think that way? The old woman was going to her own people isn't she? Now let me try and explain something.

This woman called Naomi, had left her people for a very long time. So it is possible that the people she knew and who knew her, may not be there on her return. It was also possible that even if they remembered her, no one would have time for her burden. Who takes care of an old woman except her children or a hired worker? Ruth must have thought all these out before taking the decision to go with her. Her own mother may probably be alive at that time but she thought more about Naomi.

Even though Ruth had the heart of care and thought about Naomi as a childless widow and put herself in her shoes, Naomi on her own part too had the same heart of care for Ruth. Hence this heart of care was in both women and that unknowing to them, was what brought them together in the first place. They really meant well for each other.

While Ruth cared for Naomi's wellbeing, Naomi cared about Ruth's future as a young woman. She thought to herself, who will marry her, how would she cope with staying alone with her? And with the eyes of the elders, she began to scheme, her into a program that brought them happiness together at the end. See details in Ruth chapter three as follows:

1 Then Naomi her mother in law said unto her, my daughter, shall I not seek rest for thee, that it may be well with thee? 2 And now *is* not Boaz of our kindred, with whose maidens thou wast? Behold, he winnoweth barley to night in the threshing floor. 3 Wash thy self therefore, and

anoint thee, and put thy raiment upon thee, and get thee down to the floor: *but* make not thyself known unto the man, until he shall have done eating and drinking.

4 And it shall be, when he lieth down, that thou shalt mark the place where he shall lie, and thou shalt go in, and uncover his feet, and lay thee down; and he will tell thee what thou shalt do. 5 And she said unto her, all that thou sayest unto me I will do.

What happened here is that care met care. It is loyalty and selflessness at play and the result is splendid. Ruth was loyal to her mother in-law and her mother in-law was selfless. Most mother in-laws would have been over protective and even ignored their own blessing, but Naomi was not like them.

God saw her heart and did not waste time to finish the program as scheduled. Just when you think there is no hope, God has store of hope where you are not looking. It was not long before people began to sing and dance with Naomi in celebration. They could not explain it, but the author who started it, finished it.

I am sure that Naomi must have remembered how they wept the day she asked the young lady to return back to her people and asked herself, "What if this lady, had turned back when I told her to?" I am sure too, that she thanked God over and over again, at the flash of this thought in her mind. She will first and foremost, thank God for the young lady's refusal to oblige to her order on that day and then thank Him again for giving both of them the hearts that cared for a stranger.

Again the Shunammite woman will come up in this chapter because she was also a caring woman. Her story shows how she cared for Elisha the man of God. The scripture says that she had constrained him as a stranger, to eat bread at her house and as often as he passed by, he turned in there. Then she said to her husband that she perceived that Elisha was a holy man of God.

There is no record in the story which shows, that the man of God had asked her for bread. Something in this woman hungered to do the will of God. If not, it would have been written that Elisha was hungry and went to her house to ask for bread. See how the Bible puts it in 2 kings chapter 4:

8 And it fell on a day, that Elisha passed to Shunem, where *was* a great woman; and she constrained him to eat bread. And *so* it was, that as often as he passed by, he turned in thither to eat bread. 9 And she said unto her husband, Behold now, I perceive that this is an holy man of God, which passeth by us continually. 10 Let us make a little chamber, I pray thee, on the wall; and let us set for him there a bed, and a table, and a stool, and a candlestick: and it shall be, when he cometh to us that he shall turn in thither. 11 And it fell on a day, that he came thither, and he turned into the chamber, and lay there.

There is nothing God will withhold from this woman. She only needs to ask and she will receive. Of course the record says that she was a great a woman, indicating that God had given her the blessings that makes rich and add no sorrow. Even when Elisha wanted to pray for her to have a baby, she said no to the man of God.

I think that was because God was giving her everything she needed, so she thought that if God had wanted to give her a baby too, He would have done so before then. Her life was calm. She also rejected the other offers Elisha presented to her because, she was satisfied with her life.

There is another woman of interest in Jehosheba the daughter of king Joram. This woman is recorded to have secured Joash, a Prince in Israel when Athaliah the mother of Ahaziah destroyed all, the seed royal. What Athaliah did, was to eliminate any opposition to her leadership as she took over power but Jehosheba was smart enough to steal away her brother's son and made an arrangement to keep him in safety until a later time when he became a king in Israel.

Details of this story, is recorded in the book of 2 kings chapter 11 as follows:

1 And when Athaliah the mother of Ahaziah saw that her son was dead, she arose and destroyed all, the seed royal. 2 But Jehosheba, the daughter of king Joram, sister of Ahaziah, took Joash the son of Ahaziah, and stole him from among the king's sons *which were* slain; and they hid him, *even* him and his nurse, in the bedchamber from Athaliah, so that he was not slain. 3 And he was with her hid in the house of the LORD six years. And Athaliah did reign over the land.

She saved the child because she cared. She made sure that she handed the boy and his nurse to the right people and there was no trace. There are a lot of women who if they were in her position, would not try to take such risk she took, even for their own children. You will agree with me, that Athaliah would have killed her if she found out what she did because she (Athaliah) was too desperate to accomplish her mission of taking over the kingdom and no one was going to stand on her way.

The joy Joash brought to his aunty by ruling in the fear of the Lord was very great and that made her rejoice, not regretting taking the risk she took to save him from the hands of evil Athaliah. You will also agree with me, that God will remember this record in her favor. Each time you give care, it is recorded in heaven for you. God made you a care brand and He is always watching over you to see your efforts in caring for others. It is not an option for you to care for that other person, it is a must.

It was care that Miriam the sister of Moses gave to him by standing to watch and see what would happen to him at the river. She stood there until Pharaoh's daughter picked up the basket which the boy was in and she even had the guts to go, to speak to the Princess. That was a display of boldness.

I mean what gave that little girl such guts to go and stand before the daughter of Pharaoh? She forgot that she was a slave and she was not afraid to make a suggestion to the king's daughter. I think God had arranged it, to happen the way it did. I can see God's hand writing on the story. He is always putting you in the place where you will care for someone, but the thing there is are you willing to stand in that gap?

Queen Esther's care for her uncle Mordecai is also worthy of emulation. When Mordecai tore his clothes and wore sackcloth, he came to the king's gate crying with a loud and bitter voice because of the plan that was put in place to eliminate his people. The Bible says that Esther was in great distress on hearing the news.

The record has it, that she was quick to send clothes to Mordecai and when he rejected them, she sent her attendant to go to him and enquire what the problem was. Here is how the Bible recorded it in Esther chapter 4 verses 4 and 5:

4 So Esther's maids and her chamberlains came and told it her. Then was the queen exceedingly grieved; and she sent raiment to clothe Mordecai, and to take away his sackcloth from him: but he received it not. 5 Then called Esther for Hatach, one of the king's chamberlains, whom he had appointed to attend upon her, and gave him a commandment to Mordecai, to know what it was, and why it *was*.

She wondered why her own uncle would be wearing sack clothes in a kingdom where she was a queen and she made provisions for him quickly to change what he was wearing. She may have thought, what happened to his clothes but ignored it and sent another. Her provisions were however rejected. The ordinary woman, who is not Spirit filled, would have been angry over the rejection without reasons but Esther was different. In response to the rejection, she sent someone to go and ask questions. That was care, in action.

Mary the mother of Jesus was also an interesting woman of her time when it comes to care. The visit of an angel to inform her about the birth of Jesus and her acceptance is recorded in a previous chapter of this book. She now comes up again as a caring woman because she showed it after she met with the angel. Remember, that the angel told her about one of her relation called Elizabeth and informing her that she (Elizabeth) was six months pregnant, the Bible record shows that she went to visit her and stayed with her for three months.

Three months is not three days, I guess you know? Imagine yourself going to stay with a pregnant cousin for that long. What do you think?

See the Bible details in the book of Luke chapter 1 verses 36, 39-40 and 56 below:

36 And, behold, thy cousin Elisabeth, she hath also conceived a son in her old age: and this is the sixth month with her, who was called barren. 39 And Mary arose in those days, and went into the hill country with haste, into a city of Juda; 40 And entered into the house of Zacharias, and saluted Elisabeth. 56 And Mary abode with her about three months, and returned to her own house.

I am sure, you know what it means for a young woman to visit an older pregnant woman who was in her sixth month and stayed for three months. She had gone to take care of Elizabeth until the time of her delivery and you know that pregnancy for an older woman is never easy. So Mary took all the groaning and pain cries of her cousin while she too learnt in the process.

Let me end this chapter with looking at an interesting story of women who cared for Jesus recorded in the Bible. This story is found in the book of Matthew chapter 27:

55 And many women were there beholding afar off, which followed Jesus from Galilee, ministering unto him: 56 Among which was Mary Magdalene, and Mary the mother of James and Joses, and the mother of Zebedee's children.

God had arranged the women listed above, to care for His Son while He was on earth and they followed Him everywhere He went. They saw Him crucified, but that did not discourage them. They followed to see where He was buried and went home to prepare spices with which they will visit His grave the next day. That was total care.

What else can I say? The caring woman is always highly appreciated by God. It is the will of God for the woman, to be caring. That as a matter of fact, was one of the reasons why God created her. If you look at the story of Adam and Eve again, you will see that the woman did not fail. The man failed to take care of his wife and satan stole her from him.

CHAPTER SEVEN: Obedient Woman

YE SHALL OBSERVE TO DO THEREFORE AS THE LORD YOUR GOD HATH COMMANDED YOU: YE SHALL NOT TURN ASIDE TO THE RIGHT HAND OR TO THE LEFT. YE SHALL WALK IN ALL THE WAYS WHICH THE LORD YOUR GOD HATH COMMANDED YOU, THAT YE MAY LIVE, AND *THAT IT MAY BE* WELL WITH YOU, AND *THAT* YE MAY PROLONG *YOUR* DAYS IN THE LAND WHICH YE SHALL POSSESS.

HATH THE LORD *AS GREAT* DELIGHT IN BURNT OFFERINGS AND SACRIFICES, AS IN OBEYING THE VOICE OF THE LORD? BEHOLD, TO OBEY *IS* BETTER THAN SACRIFICE, *AND* TO HEARKEN THAN THE FAT OF RAMS.

The word of God, says that you should be obedient to do what the Lord has commanded. It continued in addition that you shall neither turn to the right or to the left but you should walk strictly in the directions that the Lord commanded, so that you may live, be well and prolong your days. I think this instruction with its promises is simple. What do you think?

Let us read what God said to the children of Israel in the book of Deuteronomy chapter 28 from verses 1-14 as follow;

1 And it shall come to pass, if thou shalt hearken diligently unto the voice of the LORD thy God, to observe *and* to do all his commandments which I command thee this day, that the LORD thy God will set thee on high above all nations of the earth: 2 And all these blessings shall come on thee, and overtake thee, if thou shalt hearken unto the voice of the LORD thy God.

3 Blessed shalt thou *be* in the city, and blessed *shalt* thou *be* in the field. 4 Blessed shall be the fruit of thy body, and the fruit of thy ground, and the fruit of thy cattle, the

increase of thy kine, and the flocks of thy sheep. 5 Blessed *shall be* thy basket and thy store.

6 Blessed shalt thou be when thou comest in, and blessed shalt thou be when thou goest out. 7 The LORD shall cause thine enemies that rise up against thee to be smitten before thy face: they shall come out against thee one way, and flee before thee seven ways. 8 The LORD shall command the blessing upon thee in thy storehouses, and in all that thou settest thine hand unto; and he shall bless thee in the land which the LORD thy God giveth thee.

9 The LORD shall establish thee an holy people unto himself, as he hath sworn unto thee, if thou shalt keep the commandments of the LORD thy God, and walk in his ways. 10 And all people of the earth shall see that thou art called by the name of the LORD; and they shall be afraid of thee.

11 And the LORD shall make thee plenteous in goods, in the fruit of thy body, and in the fruit of thy cattle, and in the fruit of thy ground, in the land which the LORD sware unto thy fathers to give thee. 12 The LORD shall open unto thee his good treasure, the heaven to give the rain unto thy land

in his season, and to bless all the work of thine hand: and thou shalt lend unto many nations, and thou shalt not borrow. 13 And the LORD shall make thee the head, and not the tail; and thou shalt be above only, and thou shalt not be beneath; if that thou hearken unto the commandments of the LORD thy God, which I command thee this day, to observe and to do them: 14 And thou shalt not go aside from any of the words which I command thee this day, *to* the right hand, or to the left, to go after other gods to serve them.

Don't worry about who can do it. I know someone who can; her name is the woman who fears God. Some people ask why they should fear God and my answer is always because He is God, the superior being who is over and above all. You have just called Him God, so why ask any further questions?

You must fear Him. Do you know how you fear the traffic light on the road because you don't want to pay a fine? If only you can fear God that much, then you will be obedient to his words. Psalms 128 verses 1-2, says the following:

1 Blessed is every one that feareth the LORD; that walketh in his ways. 2 For thou shalt eat the labour of thine hands: happy shalt thou be, and it shall be well with thee.

"Do your own thing." "Have it your way." "Don't tell me what to do." These and other common phrases are used as product slogans and are often repeated by rebellious, independent individuals. For many people, it is beneath them to listen to the instruction of others. They would never think of yielding their own way of life to the will and commands of another, especially God. However, this pattern of disobedience has no place in the life of a believer.

God commanded His children to obey not just for their own benefit, but for the benefit of others, even unbelievers. As the unbeliever sees the consistent walk of obedience in the life of a believer and also begins to see the fruit it bears, they will start to ask how they can be part of it. Then the believer will have an open door to share the testimony of God's goodness, confirming what God has done for them and showing their love to God by continuing to live a life of obedience to Him.

Even though much of what true believers do may not be understood by others, people still notice the difference in their life styles. Christian often relates their obedience to how often they attend church services and other church activities, but obedience is not measured in that way. It is seen in the quiet surrendering of the matters of the heart, honesty with God, honesty with other people and especially honesty to yourself.

It also included faithfulness to yourself and your spouse, in thoughts and in action. You will spend faithful quiet times in prayer; take ample time to study and learn the word for yourself. It does not just end with relying on your own knowledge or on that of your husband's.

The obedient women believers, cultivates a heart of generosity and hospitality. They keep the home clean and orderly as an outward expression of their inner heart of obedience. When a woman believer, walks in obedience in smaller areas, God can trust her with even greater things. Obedience is therefore a key that opens the store house of God.

To obey the voice of the Lord is better than any other sacrifice you can offer to Him. There are a lot of women who have refused to walk in obedience and are running around from one prayer house to the other, where they are asked to buy one thing or another for sacrifices. Ask them, did that solve their problems?

God has given instructions which says, no adultery, no divorce, no covetousness, no gossip, no lies and many more no's and you are involved in one or all of them. How can He accept your dirty sacrifice? Don't you know that the sacrifice of a sinner is an abomination before God?

First obey what He said, repent of your sin and come to Him with a sincere heart. Refuse to be deceived, if the person who told you that you need to pray and make a sacrifice, did not tell you to stop your life style, then whatever you and that person is doing, will do or have done are never for God.

You may be deceived with the drama of shooting gun shots in the air; killing or burying goats, rams, or cows; all of it is done in obedience to the devils, which eat them and wait for a time to pass before asking for another sacrifice.

Many times, when these sacrifices people get involved with are made, things seem to become okay for them. But here is the secret, the sacrifices were made to demons and wicked spirits and they are a renewal of the covenant of your evil foundation. After these demons and wicked spirits, have enjoyed it, they keep away for some time and then they will come back for more.

See what Paul said to the Corinthians in his writing to them in 1 Corinthians chapter 10;

20 But I say, that the things which the Gentiles sacrifice, they sacrifice to devils, and not to God: and I would not that ye should have fellowship with devils. 21 Ye cannot drink the cup of the Lord, and the cup of devils: ye cannot be partakers of the Lord's table, and of the table of devils. 22 Do we provoke the Lord to jealousy? Are we stronger than he?

This is why just when you almost thought it is over, here it is again. The first round of your sacrifice has expired and the wicked gods needs another one. If you are not fast to give it to them, they will not only return you to your original status, but they will also add salt to pepper.

Jesus said, that your first state will be better than the latter because the wicked spirits will increase. Wake up woman, obey God. The Bible says in Numbers chapter 23 verses 19, "God *is* not a man that he should lie; neither the son of man, that he should repent: hath he said, and shall he not do *it*? or hath he spoken, and shall he not make it good?"

God does not lie. He does exactly what He said He will do. If God said one thing and you are doing another, how do you think He will favor you? It is better for you to say that you are not a Christian believer and follow the way of idolatry, than for you to continue pretending to be a believer and not obey God who searches the heart and understands all human intellects.

Please, read these Bible verses in Genesis chapter 3, with me:

2 And the woman said unto the serpent, we may eat of the fruit of the trees of the garden: 3 But of the fruit of the tree which *is* in the midst of the garden, God hath said, ye shall not eat of it, neither shall ye touch it, lest ye die.

From this reading, you can see that the woman (Eve) knew the truth, but the lust of the eyes took her mind away. If not that her eyes led her and she first saw, maybe she would have thought. This is the same thing that happens to most of the women of today, the lust of the eyes.

Because you need a car, a shoe, a dress, a phone and many other things that impress the eyes and give temporal satisfaction, you first see the need before any other thing. You forget the word of God and expose yourself to sexual immorality.

Some even divorce their husbands in order to satisfy their lust. What a shame. It is a big shame. Peter wrote in the book of 1 Peter chapter 3 and said the following in verses 3 and 4:

3 Whose adorning let it not be that outward adorning of plaiting the hair, and of wearing of gold, or of putting on of apparel; 4 But let it *be* the hidden man of the heart, in that which is not corruptible, even the ornament of a meek and quiet spirit, which is in the sight of God of great price.

It is the outward adorning of plaiting the hair, and of wearing of gold and of putting on of apparel, that has torn many families apart. The devil knows how important the family is to God and he has gone into so many of our families to create divisions using the women mostly because they are easily taken away by what their eyes can see.

Most women can never see anything and look away. It is always where did you make your hair? Or where did you buy the gold? Some may even buy and be in debts because they want to impress others.

David said in verses 17 of Psalms chapter 51, that the sacrifices God accepts, *is* a broken spirit. He added that God does not reject a broken and a contrite heart. That is, instead of looking for other means to please God like through sacrifices of animals, you should offer Him your heart in obedience to His will.

Only then, can He (God) change you by Himself for Himself and fill you with His Spirit. It is the Spirit of God that will convert your heart, once He comes into your life.

The symbol of the Holy Spirit is His fruit. See Galatians chapter 5 verses 22 and 23.

As the fruit of the Spirit, grows in your life you will gradually begin to see the changes you desire. There is no magic in it, the Spirit of God is the power of God to convert and rebrand. You only need to be obedient and ask Him to take over your life completely. Remember that God did not say there will be no storm. What He said, is that when you walk through the storm, He will be with you.

He will not let the storm overtake you; He will help you to walk through it and come out victoriously. So when you see a storm on the way, do not be discouraged. Always remember that your maker is by your side and develop the faith of an over-comer in obedience.

The results of total obedience to God, is always wonderful. He (God) hates disobedience. Reading through the word of God, I came across an interesting story involving Sarah and Abraham. I had used this story partly in this book, so I will just touch it briefly. It is about Sarah giving Abraham, Hagar her maid. In chapter 16 of the book of Genesis, verses 6 shows that Sarah dealt harshly with her maid after she conceived and became stubborn to her so the maid ran away. As she was in the wilderness, the angel of the Lord found her.

See the Bible details of the story from verses seven to nine below:

7 And the angel of the LORD found her by a fountain of water in the wilderness, by the fountain in the way to Shur. 8 And he said, Hagar, Sarai's maid, whence camest thou? And whither wilt thou go? And she said, I flee from the face of my mistress Sarai. 9 And the angel of the LORD, said unto her, return to thy mistress, and submits thyself under her hands.

You can agree with me, that it was God that sent the angel to Hagar and He had given the angel instructions on what to say to her, but did not mention the treatment she suffered from Sarah. Hagar was instead directed to return to her mistress and submit herself under her hand. A man would have said, let us go and see her so she will tell us why she treated you so harshly. But that is not God's way. He saw everything from the start to that point and what He wanted from Hagar towards her mistress Sarah, was total submission.

Talking about submission in this case, it actually means obedience. Without obedience, there can be no submission. Jacob had called his two wives Leah and Rachel and told them what their father had done and was doing to him. He tried to make a long explanation in order to convince them but I am sure that their response made him see, that he wasted time telling the entire story. From the answer of the women, if he had simply said let us go, they would have gone without thinking twice.

See the details of their answer in Genesis chapter thirty one from verses fourteen to sixteen below:

14 And Rachel and Leah answered and said unto him, *Is there* yet any portion or inheritance for us in our father's house? 15 Are we not counted of him strangers? For he, hath sold us and hath quite devoured also our money. 16 For all the riches which God hath taken from our father that *is* ours, and our children's: now then, whatsoever God hath said unto thee, do.

This shows the level of obedience, the women of old exhibited. They were dedicated to their marriage and will not allow anything to stand in the gap. It is not the same today. Apostle Paul in his letter to the Ephesians gave instruction to the wives concerning submission to their own husbands. He also repeated it in his letter to the Colossians. Peter in his own writing also said that submission was the way the holy women of old submitted themselves to their own husbands.

Let us look into the Bible and see the words of Paul the Apostle in his letter to the Ephesians brethren. Read Ephesians chapter 5 from verses 22 to 24 below with me:

22 Wives, submit yourselves unto your own husbands, as unto the Lord. 23 For the husband is the head of the wife, even as Christ is the head of the church: and he is the saviour of the body. 24 Therefore as the church is subject unto Christ, so let the wives be to their own husbands in everything.

When the woman submits to her husband with all her heart, she is obeying and trusting in God. She leans not on her own understanding, but sweeps it under the carpet. This woman acknowledges God in all her ways and God in return, will direct her paths. The word of God confirms this in Proverbs chapter 3 verses 5 and 6.

Though none of us likes to go through hard times, the truth is that suffering is the very thing that teaches us obedience. Even Jesus had to learn obedience through His sufferings. The scripture says, "Though He was a Son, yet He learned obedience by the things which He suffered" (Hebrews 5: 8).

His words to the Father when He was facing the cross reflect the agony He endured: "O My Father, if it is possible, let this cup pass from me; nevertheless, not as I will, but as You will" (Matthew 26:39). In spite of the pain, He surrendered completely to the Father's will.

Times of despair are tough and trying. But don't let these seasons destroy you. Allow them to refine and prepare you to fulfill your purpose and destiny. Disobedient resistance prolongs the tough times. Listen carefully to what God is saying. Daily strengthen your walk in obedience to His word.

Stay focused. Remain rooted and grounded in the faith. You will not be disappointed, for, as Paul says, "The sufferings of this present time are not worthy to be compared with the glory which shall be revealed" (Romans 8:18).

It has been said that in God's economy we can't skip grades, no matter how capable or mature we think we are. God has a lesson for us to learn in each stage of life. But His Word promises that "tribulation produces perseverance; and perseverance, character; and character, hope". And that hope, do not disappoint us (Romans 5:3-5).

Lessons in obedience are a part of our daily walk as we "grow in the grace and knowledge of our Lord and Savior Jesus Christ" (2 Peter 3:18). They are the key to finding victory over despair.

The widow of Zarephath never knew Elijah. She had made up her mind on what to do since she saw how things were going during the famine of that time. But Elijah emerged from nowhere and changed everything. This woman didn't know why what happened, happened. She just became obedient to a man she had never met anywhere in her life time because the man said, thus said the Lord.

I showed that story in a previous chapter of this book and if you can remember it, you will recollect when the woman said to Elijah, now I believe that you are a man of God and the word of God in your mouth is true. This means that even while she obeyed this strange man, she didn't believe he was a man of God until her dead son was raised back to life miraculously.

God actually sent Elijah to the widow in order to save her life and that of her son. He (God) knew her as an obedient believer and knew all that was happening to her, but He needed her to prove herself by showing obedience to a stranger this one more time so that she can confirm her status and receive the package God had sent in the care of His prophet.

The woman's past obedience was not enough to prove her stand with God. As at this time she was passing through difficulties and you know that no matter how good she was, she could have been changed by the very difficult situation she was facing at that point in time. However, this woman proved that she was still standing.

She kept her obedience even in her time of difficulties. At the point of her obedience to Elijah's request, death was her last option. She was never the less willing to listen to him and obeyed him because of God. She explained herself and her immediate situation, but after the man of God called God's name, she went ahead to provide what he asked from her.

How many people do you know, who can act like this woman? My thought is that they will be too hard to find in our today's world where a lot of people are too selfish.

During the times of despair in your life, the Lord might want to see your loyalty to Him by using the things that you may not understand. It might look like you cannot come out of your situation and while you are calling on God to help you; He is saying some strange things. Imagine you're not having money for your children's school fees and as you seek the face of God on what to do; He says begin to sing praise and worship songs to me and adds dance around your house. Now you wonder, what that has to do with what you are passing through.

Meanwhile, He (God) wants to remind you of what the essence of a real relationship with Him is. Obedience! You may have thought that it depended on what you can receive from Him and how fast they come, but He re-directs you to what He really enjoys and your obedience to His simple instructions no matter how stupid they might sound to you, is what He appreciates. With this in mind, you will begin to take a fresh look at the place of obedience to Him in your life and seek to dwell in the benefits.

There is a story in the book of 2 kings chapter 4 that I will like to make reference to. It is the story of Elisha and one of the wives of the sons of the prophet who came to him and reported that her husband was in debt before he died. Elisha told this woman to do a seemingly stupid thing. He told her, to go and borrow vessel and then use the little oil she had, to fill them. Does this sound reasonable to you? Look at the story as recorded from verses one to six;

1 Now there cried a certain woman of the wives of the sons of the prophets unto Elisha, saying, Thy servant my

husband is dead; and thou knowest that thy servant did fear the LORD: and the creditor is come to take unto him my two sons to be bondmen. 2 And Elisha said unto her, What shall I do for thee? tell me, what hast thou in the house? And she said, Thine handmaid hath not anything in the house, save a pot of oil. 3 Then he said, Go, borrow thee vessels abroad of all thy neighbours, even empty vessels; borrow not a few. 4 And when thou art come in, thou shalt shut the door upon thee and upon thy sons, and shalt pour out into all those vessels, and thou shalt set aside that which is full. 5 So she went from him, and shut the door upon her and upon her sons, who brought the vessels to her; and she poured out.

Elisha's instruction to this woman sounded like a funny drama. It would make an ordinary person laugh and roll on the floor. Tell me how a small pot of oil will be able to fill vessels? Imagine, he even told her not to borrow a few. He said that she should go abroad to borrow vessels and also ask her neighbors for more. This woman was not thinking, she trusted in the Lord and His prophet and that was why she came to Elisha in the first place. She simply obeyed what she was told and she got what she wanted.

Another story like the above is recorded in the book of 2 kings chapter 8. This one involves the Shunamite woman and Elisha. He spoke to the woman and directed her to leave because of oncoming famine and the woman obeyed. That single obedience was all it took for the woman and house hold to be fully restored after they returned from their seven years journey. Read the story from verses one to six, as written;

1 Then spake Elisha unto the woman, whose son he had restored to life, saying, Arise, and go thou and thine household, and sojourn wheresoever thou canst sojourn: for the LORD hath called for a famine; and it shall also come upon the land seven years. 2 And the woman arose, and did after the saying of the man of God: and she went with her household, and sojourned in the land of the Philistines seven years. 3 And it came to pass at the seven years' end that the woman returned out of the land of the Philistines: and she went forth to cry unto the king for her house and for her land.

4 And the king talked with Gehazi the servant of the man of God, saying, Tell me, I pray thee, all the great things that Elisha hath done. 5 And it came to pass, as he was telling

the king how he had restored a dead body to life, that, behold, the woman, whose son he had restored to life, cried to the king for her house and for her land. And Gehazi said, My lord, O king, this is the woman, and this is her son, whom Elisha restored to life. 6 And when the king asked the woman, she told him. So the king appointed unto her a certain officer, saying, Restore all that was hers, and all the fruits of the field since the day that she left the land, even until now.

See listed here, five benefits of obedience supported from the word of God. I believe they will be of benefit to you in your times of weakness.

1. Obedience makes God's faithfulness unceasing: "Therefore know that the Lord your God, He is God, the faithful God who keeps covenant and mercy for a thousand generations with those who love Him and keep His commandments" (Deuteronomy 7:9).

None of us will ever fully understand the "whys" of the troubles and issues we face. But God is faithful in responding to our love and obedience to Him. Once you have been noted by heaven for your obedience, God will never leave or forsake you. You only have to keep building your confidence in Him through His word that never changes.

2. Doors to prosperity and the pleasures of life are unlocked by obedience: "If they obey and serve Him, they shall spend their days in prosperity, and their years in pleasures" (Job 36:11).

3. Your obedience to Him makes you His special treasure: "Now therefore, if you will indeed obey My voice and keep my covenant, then you shall be a special treasure to Me above all people; for all the earth is Mine" (Exodus 19:5).

4. When you obey Him, you will have His protection: "But if you indeed obey His voice and do all that I speak, then I will be an enemy to your enemies and an adversary to your adversaries" (Exodus 23:22).

Remember this: Only those who are sensitive to the love of God can submit to the peculiar ways of God. Not everyone will understand or appreciate the anointing on your life. But praise God. No weapon formed against you will prosper!

(See Isaiah 54:17.) And when the enemy does attack, God will raise up a standard against him (Isaiah 59:19). Show me someone that failed while trusting in God and I will tell you that this someone did not obey God completely.

5. Marvelous freedom comes by walking in total obedience to God: It releases you from being concerned about the outcome. You just walk in faith and trust God to handle things.

CHAPTER EIGHT: Wise Woman

> **EVERY WISE WOMAN BUILDETH HER HOUSE: BUT THE FOOLISH PLUCKETH IT DOWN WITH HER HANDS.**

The scripture is clear about wisdom and the need for you to get it. This is why it states that it is the wise woman that builds her house while the foolish pulls down her own house with her hands. Wisdom is further addressed as a "She" in the book of proverbs. So it is appropriate for the woman to have her.

The writer of the book of Proverbs addressed her as more precious than rubies and all the things you can desire cannot be compared to her. It is also stated that length of days are in her right hand. In her left hands are riches and honor. Pleasantness is in her ways, all her paths are peace. She is a tree of life to them that lay hold on her and happy is everyone that keeps her. This goes to show how important it is to God, for you to get wisdom. The scripture gives an authoritatively directive that says, get wisdom. It warns, that you must not forsake her because she preserves. Love her and she shall keep you.

Wisdom is called a principal thing in proverbs chapter 4 verses 7. In verses 8 and 9 of the same chapter of the book of Proverbs, it is written that when you exalt her, she will promote you and she will bring you to honour, when you embrace her. It concludes that she shall give to your head an ornament of grace and deliver a crown of glory to you. These statements are too powerful to ignore.

A wise woman does not take anything for granted. She is thankful to be loved and seeks to make herself, lovelier. A wise woman doesn't allow herself to be a liability but strives to be an asset to the marriage bond. She looks for ways to make, save, and use money wisely.

Her husband knows he is a richer man because she is his wife. She seeks to be a part of her husband's life. His interest becomes her interest. She looks for ways to help him in every endeavor in which he is involved. When he needs a helping hand, it is her hand that is there first.

A wise woman knows that her peace of mind (and sometimes, wise understanding) is something she can give or take away by her observations and conversation concerning circumstances or people. She limits her conversation to the positive and stays away from negative people who might want to influence her thoughts and gossip about other people.

She sets a joyful mood in the household and uses laughter, music and happy times to stir the children to a positive, joyful frame of mind. She knows this light-heartedness helps take stress off her husband and their children experiences peace in the home.

A wise woman gauges her husband's needs. She seeks to fulfill his desires before even he is aware of them. She never leaves him daydreaming outside the home. She supplies his every desire. She understands her husband's need to be honored. It is not based on his performance but on his position, as her head.

She learns quickly to defer with enthusiasm to his ideas or plans. She looks for ways to reverence him because she knows its God's will for her life.

A wise woman is not pitiful, puny, or whiny. She seeks to be confident, capable and thankful. She does not dream of what "could have been." She sees clearly that she's God's gift to men; thus she is blessed in her present circumstances. She learns to be content. She never expects anyone to serve her; therefore she is never disappointed. She is ready to help—a giver. By her example her children learn to serve cheerfully and energetically.

A wise woman doesn't attempt to instruct her husband through feigned questions. Her questions are sincere inquiries concerning his will. She is always learning. She is open to change. She is ready to hear. She wants to know. She doesn't cloud her mind with the foolish folly of entertainment. She uses her time wisely.

Rahab was a wise woman. She saw an opportunity to save herself and her family and took it. But it did not come without an effort, from her own side. She needed to secure the men that ran into her place because she saw, that they can reciprocate her assistance when they returned to take over Jericho.

It takes a lot of wisdom to overcome a situation like the one Rahab was in on that particular day and God gave it to her. Imagine a woman having to use a cord to let two men down through a window? That was what she did. The record says, that she let them down by a cord through the window: for her house was on the town wall, and she dwelt on the wall. And she told them to go to the mountain and hide themselves there, for three days until the pursuers returned and then they can go their way.

That was wisdom at play. If she could not do what she did, there was no other way for the men to get out of Jericho. She also told the men to hide themselves for three days so that their pursuers can go on their pursuit and return. Note that she had sent them to the roof of the house at the first instance. Her head was on fire as all this were going on. She needed to make sure, that it all came out good in order to achieve her heart desire and it did.

I see another woman of wisdom in Abigail. I told her story as it written in the book of 1 Samuel chapter 25, in that story, Abigail was introduced as the wife of a wealthy man named Nabal (which means "fool"). She is also a woman of good understanding and beautiful. I love how she is described first as being "sensible", "intelligent" and "discerning" depending on which translation you read.

This woman was so wise that David fell in love with her on meeting her for the first time. What David saw, was a woman one can leave at home and feel at peace wherever you are because she can control anything left under her care.

Abigail was probably married to Nabal through an arranged marriage. The marriage must have been based on his wealth, rather than in his character. We are not told how long she was married to him but she knew him well enough and knew too that for his scorning David, he and their household will reap disaster.

She sets off quickly to meet David without her husband's knowledge, knowing that he would only stop her from trying to make amends to what he had done. Like a virtuous woman, she opened her mouth with wisdom when she met David and in her tongue was the law of kindness.

When you make foolish choices, the ones where your judgments are off and makes your actions off, you invite pain, guilt, and heartbreak because you are unwilling to see what is true. This is especially true of single women who are tired of the waiting and settle for unequally yoked relationships.

I cannot tell you how much heartbreak and tears I have heard from people who have settled for less than God's best and paid such a steep price. Everything from their loss of relationship with God to losing their ministry, are filled with regrets. They always say, had I known. But by then, it's too late.

The story of Abigail is similar to that of the people of Israel making a golden calf. You can read about it in Exodus chapter 32. Aaron was left alone with God's people while Moses spoke with God on Mt. Sinai. The people became restless and anxious for direction since their leader was still away. They asked their new priest Aaron to make them a god for them to follow.

Aaron instructed them to get all the gold earrings and with it, he created a molten calf. From the mountain where God was with Moses, His anger was kindled against the nation of Israel. So much so that He wanted to "consume" them with His wrath and start over again with Moses.

The Israelites were "stiff necked" just like Nabal – foolish in their understanding and incredibly impatient. Moses pleased God just as Abigail did with David. Both God's anger and David's anger could only be diffused by reminding them of the greatness that was to come. For God, it would be a nation of many just as the stars in the sky. For David, it would be a promised kingdom with no end.

In the midst of wrong doings, judging and acting correctly helps to diffuse the most heated situations. Looking at Abigail, you can see the fruit of having wisdom in your life. I want to bring it out here for your use in preparing yourself to become God's love and they are listed as follows:

Humbleness: Abigail humbled herself before David, the future king of Israel.

Intercession: Abigail brought food for him to eat, which Nabal refused to do. You can be a women who stands in the gap for your lost loved ones because you know a relationship with Jesus gives joy, peace, wholeness, and so much more.

Pleasing God: Abigail reminded David of the big story picture while David was focusing on the slight of the present. She reminded him that killing Nabal would be a spot on his record.

Evidence of fruitfulness and beauty: The same word that is used for wisdom is used for the creativity God gave the workers of the first temple in the desert. The Holy Spirit inspired these men to work metals and woods like never before and they produced such expert beauty. Wisdom produces a beauty to our lives that others have to stop and listen.

Remember the queen of Sheba mentioned in the book of 2 Chronicle chapter 9. This woman merely heard about the Wisdom of Solomon and travelled all the way from her country to visit him. Such visit can be said to have been triggered by the desire for impartation. Jesus also spoke about her in Matthew chapter 12 verses 42, saying the following:

"The queen of the south shall rise up in the judgment with this generation, and shall condemn it: for she came from the uttermost parts of the earth to hear the Wisdom of Solomon; and, behold, a greater than Solomon is here".

What was the quest of this queen of the South? She did not take her long journey for vanity or out of any feminine curiosity because she had heard of the much heralded greatness of Solomon. Hers was not a State visit to make a new treaty of some sort or to behold the magnificence of the court of Solomon. No, she was a seeker after wisdom and so made the tedious journey from her own palace to that of Solomon's to increase her knowledge.

She was inspired to make the visit because the fame of Solomon as the wisest man in the East had reached her. The Bible distinctly says that "she came to prove Solomon with hard, or perplexing questions," and her questions were both numerous and varied. This nameless queen had heard that Solomon knew all about "the name of the Lord," and it was this particular aspect of his wisdom that attracted her to Jerusalem.

She had not come to see the king's material possessions and trappings of wealth, for as a queen of considerable importance she had plenty of this herself. She came to see and hear "the Wisdom of Solomon," as Christ said of her.

As, centuries later, wise men came from the East to Bethlehem to worship Him who appeared as, "the Wisdom of God," so Sheba's queen came to the Holy City in search of higher knowledge. She was not only a woman of enterprise and affluence but also of a penetrating mind. Cultured, she had a thirst for wider intellectual pursuits, and therefore represented the desire in the hearts of all princely characters for a deeper understanding of the true knowledge.

The story of the Shunammite woman which I have used repeatedly in this book has everything to do with wisdom. This woman will be called wise because she was discerning. She discerned that Elisha was a holy man of God and keyed into his blessings. It was wisdom that made her act the way she did, when her son died. She simply saddled a donkey and headed to the prophet. She kept on saying it is well until she got to the man of God and fell at his feet.

Wisdom teaches you how to be in control of situations around you. Even when it seems like the end has come, a wise individual will always be in a better position to know, what to do or how to apply an idea in order to solve a seemingly difficult problem. It is wisdom that opens your eye of understanding and even though your act might be seen as stupid by someone around you; at the end of the day it will become an appreciated solution to whatever the situation may be.

Let us see the woman introduced as a wise woman in 2 Samuel chapter 20 verses 16:

"Then cried a wise woman out of the city, hear, hear; say, I pray you, unto Joab, Come near hither, that I may speak with thee".

The story here is that a man who committed a crime against the king of Israel had run into a city where this wise woman lived and disaster was on its way to the city. Joab the commander in chief of the armed forces had come after the man in question, ready for war. This woman however, was wise enough not to allow such disaster into her city.

She therefore volunteered herself to meet Joab outside the city and demanded to know what, was the problem. When Joab saw her wisdom, he explained to her what had brought him and this woman acted wisely. Her action is described in verses 22 of that chapter, as follows:

"Then the woman went unto all the people in her wisdom. And they cut off the head of Sheba the son of Bichri, and cast it out to Joab. And he blew a trumpet, and they retired from the city, every man to his tent. And Joab returned to Jerusalem unto the king".

What a heart of courage? Bichri was the source of disaster and this woman knew what to do. Jesus advised us to remove whatever might stop us from entering into the Kingdom of God. Something just came to your mind, yes, that's right, cut it off!

The scripture says that the woman with the issue of blood thought in her heart that if she touched the helm of the garment of Jesus, she will be healed. She thought it in her heart; she did not discuss it with anyone. That is wisdom. She knew how men are and did not want to be discouraged.

She needed to do just what her heart told her to do and she convinced herself, that it will be well with her. If she had told her friends, maybe she would have died in her sickness because they would have discouraged her against doing what she did. She took a wise decision by herself and went to touch as she had thought in her heart. It worked for her, didn't it?

Wisdom is keeping that your new idea, that your new plan, that your dream and visions, that your secret to yourself until they manifest. You can never tell who has bad thoughts towards you. Yes I know she is your sister, yes I know she is your best friend and you never kept anything from each other, but what you don't understand is that you and this person has always been on the same level and that is why you have not had problems. Wait until it looks like you are moving ahead.

Mary and Martha were the sisters of Lazarus and this man Lazarus was a friend of Jesus. When Lazarus was sick, the sisters invited his friend Jesus to come and pray for him. I had told this story, but what I am trying to bring out here again is the wisdom that was in Mary.

Martha had met with Jesus when He came and because to her, he came late, she was not happy since Lazarus was dead already. No matter what Jesus said to console her, she continued to show unhappiness. At one point, she just left Jesus and went to call her sister Mary, to come and see Him. The Bible recorded what happened in the book of John chapter 11: 32-34.

When Mary came to where Jesus was, and saw him, she fell down at his feet, saying to him, Lord, if you had been here, my brother would not have died. She wept and Jesus saw her weeping. The Jews which came with her, also wept. Immediately, Jesus groaned in the spirit and was troubled. And said, "Where have ye laid him"? They told him, to come and see. Then Jesus wept.

When Mary came to Jesus, she fell at His feet and began to weep. Now what she did here was to pull His garment. The other woman touched a part of His garment, but Mary pulled on the entire garment. Not physically, but spiritually. Immediately, Jesus asked, where did you bury him? The scripture recorded that Jesus wept. You can agree with me that what made Him (Jesus) weep was the wisdom that Mary applied.

She had said exactly what her sister said when she met Jesus, but her approach was different. That's wisdom at play and God loves it. You must get wisdom if you must impress God to respond to your needs and this wisdom is a gift. Ask God for it today and receive it in Jesus Christ name, Amen!

CHAPTER NINE: Courageous Woman

> BE STRONG AND OF A GOOD COURAGE, FEAR NOT, NOR BE AFRAID OF THEM: FOR THE LORD THY GOD, HE *IT IS* THAT DOTH GO WITH THEE; HE WILL NOT FAIL THEE, NOR FORSAKE THEE.

Every woman of courage has a place with God. The Bible has records of women who showed courage in their walk with God and they were not disappointed. If God said be of good courage and fear not, then He meant it. The word of God added that He will go with you and will not fail or forsake you. Understanding and trusting completely in God, is what gives courage. You must be in a position where you agree with God in everything He said and He is saying, accept it in your heart that He is able to fulfill His word.

I will say that Sarah, the wife of Abraham was a very courageous woman. When God called her husband and told him to leave his father's house and go to the place He (God) will send him, the Bible says that he (Abraham) took his wife Sarah with him and she demonstrated faith and obedience while believing God's promises. She left her comfortable and familiar surroundings to launch her journey with God.

She did not know where they were going, but she knew that her husband had heard God. One may ask if that was enough for her to join him without asking any question. But you must understand, that her husband must have told her all that God had said to him. It is then her accepting the word that God spoke to her husband and complying with it, without fear that is courage.

You may know that before the time Abraham met God, he never knew Him. He may have heard that there is superior being somewhere, but never or family members never knew Him. They were idol worshippers and had manmade gods that they worshipped. Many women in the shoes of Sarah would have tried to convince their husbands to think twice. She would have asked him, if was going to leave the gods his father's worshipped?

Two times in their journey, Sarah was taken by kings who saw her with her husband and liked her. These kings took her home to become their wife after she had agreed with her husband to say that he was her brother. She had confidence in the God her husband had found and became friends with.

There were lots of what ifs in these stories, but in all of them, Sarah was very courageous and stood her ground in all of it. The seemingly difficult circumstances they passed through in their journey, helped to build her faith in God. Imagine God showing up each time it looked like it was over? She would have told herself, "This is the God, I will serve forever".

Now there were two women in the time of Pharaoh king of Egypt, who were very courageous. Their names are given in the Bible as Shiphrah and Puah. It is not clear which nationality they were. Some think that they may have been Hebrews because, why would Egyptian midwives spare the lives of the Hebrew children? They were probably not the only two midwives in Egypt, but their courage is very remarkable.

There were millions of people in Egypt and these two midwives would not have been sufficient especially for this burgeoning Hebrew population. It is likely that the two women were in charge of a national network of midwives throughout the land of Egypt.

The Bible recorded that a Pharaoh rose, who knew not Joseph and started treating the children of Israel harshly. According to what is written, the king complained that the population of the children of Israel was increasing and he therefore made plans to reduce them. The details of this story, is recorded in the book of Exodus chapter 1 as follows:

8 Now there arose up a new king over Egypt, which knew not Joseph. 9 And he said unto his people, Behold, the people of the children of Israel *are* more and mightier than we: 10 Come on, let us deal wisely with them; lest they multiply, and it come to pass, that, when there falleth out any war, they join also unto our enemies, and fight against us, and *so* get them up out of the land. 11 Therefore they

did set over them taskmasters to afflict them with their burdens. And they built for Pharaoh treasure cities, Pithom and Raamses.

12 But the more they afflicted them, the more they multiplied and grew. And they were grieved because of the children of Israel. 13 And the Egyptians made the children of Israel to serve with rigour: 14 And they made their lives bitter with hard bondage, in mortar, and in brick, and in all manner of service in the field: all their service, wherein they made them serve, was with rigour.

15 And the king of Egypt spake to the Hebrew midwives, of which the name of the one *was* Shiphrah, and the name of the other Puah: 16 And he said, When ye do the office of a midwife to the Hebrew women, and see them upon the stools; if it be a son, then ye shall kill him: but if it be a daughter, then she shall live. 17 But the midwives feared God, and did not as the king of Egypt commanded them, but saved the men children alive.

18 And the king of Egypt called for the midwives, and said unto them, Why have ye done this thing, and have saved the men children alive? 19 And the midwives said unto

Pharaoh, because the Hebrew women are not as the Egyptian women; for they are lively, and are delivered ere the midwives come in unto them. 20 Therefore God dealt well with the midwives: and the people multiplied, and waxed very mighty.

Now these midwives were likely slaves themselves and the king who gave them this directive held absolute authority over their lives. But look at what verse 17, tells us about these midwives. "But the midwives feared God and did not do as the king of Egypt commanded them, but let the male children live." That's an incredible action.

Here is Pharaoh, the most powerful man in the world, issuing an edict. He said, kill the boys and these two ordinary midwives said, "We won't do it." What a courage?

You see, these women feared God more than they feared what Pharaoh could do to them. They were more concerned about God's wrath, which will last for eternity, than they were about Pharaoh's threats. I guess they thought, what more could Pharaoh do, than kill them? He couldn't do anything else to them other than to kill their bodies. They feared God who kills the body and destroys the soul, more than they feared the king of Egypt.

As I pondered over this passage of the Bible, I came to really admire these two women. They stand in a long line of many women who reverenced God and had said we will not bow to any other god except the God of creation. If the word of the king contradicts the Word of God, we ought to obey God rather than man. The fear of God is what encouraged these women and delivered them from the fear of man.

The other courageous women I will like to bring in here; are the five daughters of Zelophehad. Their story is the book of Numbers chapter 27 verses 1-8. These girls; Mahlah, Noah, Hoglah, Milcah and Tirzah stood fearless and firm and as a result reformed the culture of their day. Because they spoke up, they reversed precedent and claimed possession of their father's inheritance.

See the details of their story as follows:

1 Then came the daughters of Zelophehad, the son of Hepher, the son of Gilead, the son of Machir, the son of

Manasseh, of the families of Manasseh the son of Joseph: and these *are* the names of his daughters; Mahlah, Noah, and Hoglah, and Milcah, and Tirzah. 2 And they stood before Moses, and before Eleazar the priest, and before the princes and all the congregation, by the door of the tabernacle of the congregation, saying,

3 Our father died in the wilderness, and he was not in the company of them that gathered themselves together against the LORD in the company of Korah; but died in his own sin, and had no sons. 4 Why should the name of our father be done away from among his family, because he hath no son? Give unto us therefore a possession among the brethren of our father.

5 And Moses brought their cause before the LORD. 6 And the LORD spoke unto Moses, saying, 7 The daughters of Zelophehad speak right: thou shalt surely give them a possession of an inheritance among their father's brethren; and thou shalt cause the inheritance of their father to pass unto them. 8 And thou shalt speak unto the children of Israel, saying, if a man die, and have no son, then ye shall cause his inheritance to pass unto his daughter.

When Moses saw their courage, he had to take their case to God and God responded positively in favor of the girls. God said that they spoke right and directed Moses to give them a possession of an inheritance among their father's brethren.

He told Moses to pass the inheritance of their father to them and added that he should speak to the children of Israel informing them that if a man dies and have no son, then his inheritance should be passed to his daughters. You can see what courage can do?

The girls were speaking for themselves, not knowing that they were about to bring an important change in the culture of a people. Does that teach you something? Stop being silent, it might be that it is your voice that will save others. You must speak out today.

Ruth, the Moabite was able to overcome her past by giving her life over to the living God. By turning from her idolatrous way of life, she was able to put herself in a position where she was used mightily of the Lord as the great grandmother of king David. She was so courageous that she forgot her own people and followed an old woman who was her mother in-law and went with her to another country. Of course you know that Jesus came through the linage of David.

This woman (Ruth); stood her ground in courage. I have told her story in the chapters of this book and if you can remember, even her mother in-law advised her to return to her people but she refused. She was encouraged in the Lord to follow Naomi. Did she only follow? No. She followed with a promise she made to the woman, saying where you go I will go, where you leave I will leave, where you die I will die, where you are buried, I will be buried, your people will become my people, your God will become my God and may God do this and that to me if not only death shall separate us.

What else do you think can make this young woman make such statements but courage? You must note that she said, your God will be my God. This goes to show that this idolatrous woman was at that point, holding on to God. She knew this God through her marriage to a family of God who taught her. Her head was filled with the stories of a glorious God who never fails and she was following Him.

Let me talk about Priscilla. This woman ministered the gospel together with her husband Aquila. The Bible describes her as an effective mentor, when she and her husband took Apollos aside and explained to him the way of God more accurately. Courage is what gives strength to minister to others and Priscilla had it. That was why she was able to minister in the company of her husband. The details of their story showed that their meeting with Apollos was not too long after they stayed with Apostle Paul.

The two returned from Italy and because Paul had the same craft with them, he stayed in their house and made tents with them. I am of the opinion that their stay with him helped them to develop courage in the Lord. I guess that while they were together, Paul encouraged them with the word of God and as they heard him speak in the synagogue, they themselves grew day by day. What they shared with Apollos was what they heard from Paul and their sharing it without fear, showed their courage.

After Mary Magdalene was delivered from a life of demonic oppression, she followed Jesus and became the first woman that experienced His resurrected power. Her courage is recorded in the scriptures but the book of John chapter 20 gave detailed information on how it all happened. The story of this Mary has appeared almost on all the chapters of this book, using her as an example of a woman who feared God and showing how much God loved her. Her courage was stronger than that of the Apostles of Jesus.

Once when Jesus visited her and her sister Martha, she stayed with the Lord while her sister ran around to prepare food for their visitor. Martha complained to Jesus but see the answer He gave to her as written in Luke chapter 10;

41 And Jesus answered and said unto her, Martha, Martha, thou art careful and troubled about many things: 42 But one thing is needful: and Mary hath chosen that good part, which shall not be taken away from her.

I want to assume that by now, you are learning how to build up yourself and become the courageous woman of your generation. You have seen that it all begins through a relationship with the Lord. These women of the Bible I have mentioned this book so far, did great exploits through their listening and hearing the word of God, believing in it and following what they heard in obedience.

Courage is what it takes to become everything God destined you to become in life. To be faithful, you need courage. To pray according to the will of God, you need courage. To wait for God's answer, you need courage. So you see that without being courageous, you cannot achieve results in your walk with God because He follows your heart and loves to see your sincere dedication to Him.

Another woman in the Bible who through courage obtained a good report from God is Hannah. I have also told her story in previous chapters of this book. According to the scripture, she prayed fervently and made a vow to the Lord that if He gave her a male child, she will give him back to Him. Looking again at that story, I believe her prayer was triggered by an event that occurred in the Shiloh environment.

I say this because it was not her first time there at Shiloh with her husband. They have been going there yearly, to worship and make sacrifices to the Lord of Host, but this time that she prayed her prayer, was different.

My thought is that may be, during their stay at Shiloh that year, someone gave a testimony of how God answered her own prayer after she prayed and made a vow and that testimony got Hannah's attention. She was encouraged by it and so she decided to pray like the testifier and God also answered her own prayer to teach another person that courageous and persistent prayer gets His attention. This is just my thought.

What I am trying to bring out here, is that Hannah must have heard something new about the goodness of God and what she heard gave her just the box of courage she needed. While she prayed, the chief priest saw her. He noticed that her mouth moved, but he did not hear what she was saying. This made him think, she was drunk and he spoke to advise her against drinking saying, "How long wilt thou be drunken? Put away thy wine from thee".

Hannah answered to counter the thought of the priest by saying, "No, my lord, I am a woman of a sorrowful spirit: I have drunk neither wine nor strong drink, but have poured out my soul before the LORD. Count not thine handmaid for a daughter of Belial: for out of the abundance of my complaint and grief have I spoken hitherto".

Reading through this story, you will see that it was Hannah who went alone and prayed to God. Her husband was not there with her as at the time she made a vow to God, so it must not have been easy for her to tell her husband that she vowed to give her first child back to God. This was another side where her courage is noted. See below how the scripture recorded it in the following verses of 1 Samuel chapter 1;

20 Wherefore it came to pass, when the time was come about after Hannah had conceived, that she bare a son, and called his name Samuel, saying, Because I have asked him of the LORD. 21 And the man Elkanah, and all his house, went up to offer unto the LORD the yearly sacrifice, and his vow. 22 But Hannah went not up; for she said unto her husband, I will not *go up* until the child be weaned, and *then* I will bring him, that he may appear before the LORD, and there abide forever.

I am sure her husband must have asked what she meant and she told him. The statement her husband made in response does not show that he was as courageous as the woman. He said; do what seems best to you, stay until you have weaned him; only let God do what is good. Do you see what I mean? It seems to me like his heart was not really in agreement with his wife, but he had to let it be since God was involved.

The Samaritan woman met Jesus at the well and became one of the first mass evangelists for Jesus Christ. She was able to confront her past truthfully and transform into a motivating mouthpiece for the Lord. She had come to the well to get water alone but on getting there, she saw Jesus sitting by the well. She realized that He was a Jew and knowing that the Jews had no dealings with the Samaritans, she was courageous to ask Him why He asked her for a drink. It was this question that opened up a discussion between them.

When Jesus asked her to go and call her husband, the woman again showed courage by answering I have no husband. If that question was a test, she passed. Someone else may have asked why He wanted her to bring her husband or what her husband has to do with their meeting. But it was not so with this woman. Even when she did not know who she was dealing with, she held her courage by being honest with the Lord. She asked Jesus some questions when he proverbially introduced Himself to her as the living water. That was another sign of courage. She said to Him, you have nothing to draw with and asked, from where will you get the living water? Are you greater than our father Jacob?

The answers Jesus gave to her questions were too powerful for her to understand but even in her confusion, she was courageous to say, to him; "Give me this water that I may thirst no more nor come here again to draw". She was thirsty for the living water. She is the type of people, God is looking for. Those who hunger and thirst after righteousness.

The discussion Jesus had with this woman on that day including questions and answer, were enough to encourage her more strongly and she spoke boldly. And that was she immediately went into the city, to spread the good news about Jesus to everybody. She said, He told her everything she ever did and the people believed her because they noticed something different about her.

They knew that whatever had touched her was powerful, so they all came out to see who she was talking about. The whole people accepted Jesus because one woman was courageous and stood before Him. That is the kind of woman God loves. She refused to be limited by the situation around her and broke into victory through courage.

You can become like this woman. As you read this her story, you are also at the well just as the woman came on that day and Jesus sat by the side. I hope you can see Him, asking you to give Him water to drink? Do not say no to Him. Instead be ready to open up yourself to Him and let Him have all of your heart. What are you waiting for, open your mouth and speak to Him right now. He is waiting to answer your many questions and bring satisfaction to you.

Esther modeled bravery and courage, when she risked her life to save the lives of her people. She teaches us that we must break intimidation and use our influence to bring glory to God. This woman as a young queen was faced with the challenge of saving her people under a life threatening circumstance. If not for the courage she had in the Lord, she would not have been able to do what she did. She knew it was risky, yet she ventured into it because she trusted in the Lord.

Courage was all it took to implement her plans one step at a time. She took courage to go to the king after she had fasted for three days and he accepted her. Upon the king asking to know what she wanted, she requested that the enemy of the Jews should be invited to a banquet she prepared and it was granted. Haman came to the banquet and when they had finished eating, the king asked Esther again what she wanted but she was courageous enough to postponed, her request until after they have eaten another banquet she prepared.

She knew the word of God that says, "God is able to make all grace abound toward you; that ye, always having all sufficiency in all things, may abound to every good work". And so she was not afraid. Did it work? Yes it did. This is called unlimited courage.

The story of Jael in Judges Chapter 4 shows another woman of courage. This woman's courageous heart led her to do what only an exceptional woman can do. She knew the trouble that was going to come upon her people because of a man who had ran into her house due to defeat in war and she took it upon herself to solve that problem, by killing the man with a nail and a hammer. She did not take instruction from anyone.

See her story from verses seventeen to twenty two;

17 Howbeit Sisera fled away on his feet to the tent of Jael the wife of Heber the Kenite: for *there was* peace between Jabin the king of Hazor and the house of Heber the Kenite. 18 And Jael went out to meet Sisera, and said unto him, Turn in, my lord, turn in to me; fear not. And when he had turned in unto her into the tent, she covered him with a mantle.

19 And he said unto her, Give me, I pray thee, a little water to drink; for I am thirsty. And she opened a bottle of milk, and gave him drink, and covered him. 20 Again he said unto her, Stand in the door of the tent, and it shall be, when any man doth come and inquire of thee, and say, is there any man here? That thou shalt say, No.

21 Then Jael Heber's wife took a nail of the tent, and took an hammer in her hand, and went softly unto him, and smote the nail into his temples, and fastened it into the ground: for he was fast asleep and weary. So he

died. 22 And, behold, as Barak pursued Sisera, Jael came out to meet him, and said unto him, come, and I will show thee the man whom thou seekest. And when he came into her *tent*, behold, Sisera lay dead, and the nail *was* in his temples.

She actually went out to beckon on this man to come to her, so she could kill him. Her mind was made up on what to do and she took courage in the Lord to do it. You can understand that killing with a hammer and nail is not as easy as pulling the trigger of a gun. Deborah the Prophetess sang a song in Judges Chapter 5: 24-27, saying the following;

24 Blessed above women shall Jael the wife of Heber the Kenite be, blessed shall she be above women in the tent.
25 He asked water, and she gave him milk; she brought forth butter in a lordly dish. 26 She put her hand to the nail and her right hand to the workmen's hammer; and with the hammer she smote Sisera, she smote off his head, when she had pierced and stricken through his temples. 27 At her feet he bowed, he fell, he lay down: at her feet he bowed, he fell: where he bowed, there he fell down dead.

Deborah, who was the Prophetess and Judge to Israel during that time, was also known for her wisdom, courage and compassionate zeal for justice. She had called on Barak the son of Abinoam out of Kedeshnaphtali to embark on the war that brought honor to Jael, but Barak insisted that she should go with him or he will not go. And she said I will surely go with you. She added that notwithstanding, the journey shall not be to the honor of Barak because the Lord had sold Sisera into the hand of a woman. And Deborah arose, and went with Barak to Kedesh.

She was not afraid to go to war. You can agree with me, that it's not every woman that will have the courage to go to a battle front as Deborah did. As a Prophetess and a Judge in Israel, she had every reason not to go to the war with Barak, but she went. I believe she encouraged herself in the Lord as one who carried His word. She had told Barak that the Lord had delivered Sisera, his chariots and his multitude into his hands but he thought to himself, if she was sure of the word God spoke to him through her why should she, not go with him.

What courage does; is to eliminate every form of fear that might want to stand on your way. It makes sure that you make up your mind and once your mind is made up to do the right thing, you don't get discouraged on the way. Ask yourself what you have always thought is good for you to do, but you have not done it because you are afraid. Pick courage and step out to try. Who said you cannot do it? This might be the time for it.

I am sure you remember Miriam, the sister of Moses. She came up in the book of Exodus chapter 2 and displayed a remarkable courage, intelligence and confidence. She did not only help to save her brother's life, she also helped to set Israel's deliverance in motion through her courage at the time Pharaoh's daughter picked Moses at the river. She stood by the side of the river, to see what would happen to her brother and when she saw that he was picked by the king's daughter, she came out and played a very vital role.

Her courage at that time was wonderful. While she was alone and watched over her brother, she was filled with thoughts on how best she could save him if the need arose. She may have thought of herself as a woman who might be able to do anything. But as she was thinking, the king's daughter appeared and picked up the child from the river. Immediately, Miriam was encouraged to take a quick action. She began by approaching Pharaoh's daughter and her first action was to speak. Yes, she opened her mouth and asked a question. She was not afraid to play this part. Though it was risky, she was expectant and courage gave her the answer she got.

You can understand with me at this point that courage always springs up in risky situations. Until someone is willing to take risks, courage never wakes up. It is waiting for you to arise and stand in the gap for your people and others. Let courage lead you to pray in a way that no one else has ever prayed before. Not for yourself or your family but for those who don't even know that you are praying for them.

Your generation is waiting for you to break forth and bring the change that is required to re-shape the future. The time is now, so begin to make your move.

CHAPTER TEN: Discerning Woman

> BELOVED, DO NOT BELIEVE EVERY SPIRIT, BUT TEST THE SPIRITS TO SEE WHETHER THEY ARE FROM GOD, FOR MANY FALSE PROPHETS HAVE GONE OUT INTO THE WORLD...THEREFORE THEY SPEAK FROM THE WORLD, AND THE WORLD LISTENS TO THEM.

The scripture makes it absolutely clear that the times are indeed coming, and have already come, when false teachers will appear on the scene and lead many well-intentioned people astray. Therefore without a consistent, Spirit-led growth in Biblical and gospel-centered discernment, many Christians are susceptible to confusion, deceit, and blindness. Look around you and you will see what is going on.

The English word, "discern," comes from the Greek word "anakrino" which means to distinguish, to separate out by diligent search, or to examine.

Discernment is the mother, the guardian and the guide of all the virtues. It is essential in the life of a believer. Every day we make countless decisions both big and small like what you will eat, wear, say, where you will go, how you will spend your money, how you will spend your time, what you will watch or listen to and what you believe.

The scripture says, that we have not received the spirit of the world, but the spirit which is of God; that we might know the things that are freely given to us of God. Which things also we speak, not in the words which man's wisdom teaches, but which the Holy Ghost teaches; comparing spiritual things with spiritual. But the natural man receives not the things of the Spirit of God: for they are foolishness to him: neither can he know them, because they are spiritually discerned. (1 Corinthians 2: 12-14).

Discernment helps you to judge rightly, see clearly and understand spiritual things. It is like a spiritual filter that separates dark, dirty lies from sweet, liberating truth.

Discernment serves as a sieve to divide the destructive from the constructive; that which builds up from that which tears down. Discernment simply allows us to know the difference between what is good and what is best. So, how do we get this handy-dandy discernment to help us wisely deal with all the influences we face?

1. Ask for it.

First, you just have to ask God for it through prayer, "I am your servant; give me discernment that I may understand your statutes" (Psalm 119:125) Just as you ask someone to give you a ride or give you what you need, you ask God to give you discernment. He gives it to you, by His Holy Spirit. The Bible tells us that God's Word is "spiritually discerned." Without the Holy Spirit's discernment, the things of God are "foolishness". They make no sense at all. See (1 Corinthians 2:14).

To be a woman of discernment, ask God for it and then apply it. We ask God for discernment just as we ask Him for wisdom. "If any of you lacks wisdom, let him ask God, who gives generously to all without reproach, and it will be given him." (James 1:5). So, if you find yourself in dilemmas and you are not sure of what is right or what is wrong, if you feel like you are easily influenced, ask God for discernment. It is a gift that the Holy Spirit gives freely to the hungry.

2. Apply it.

Secondly, once you have asked for it, you just need to believe that you have got it and begin to exercise your mind as someone God came by and packed plenty of the Spirit of discernment within. Go for it. Just apply it in your daily life in the ordinary places.

Now, before you begin to read, ask God to give you discernment to recognize what is truth and what is lies; what is right and what is wrong. Ask Him to guide you to see what influences you toward faith and what draws you from it. Ask Him to reveal what brings you life and growth and what brings you down and leads to stinking thinking. This world needs an army of discerning women to be a bright influence in the dark.

When we bring our best to the world, we will bring out the best in our world. Practice that same kind of discernment throughout your day as you listen to people, read or anything else you are involved with. This world needs an army of discerning women to be a big, bright influence in all the dark, dingy places where there is no light. Rather than being women who are influenced by things that don't bring out their best, let them be women of influence through discernment. It is then that women will bring the best to their world and bring out the best in the world.

The two midwives (Shiphrah and Puah), were the people Pharaoh gave instruction concerning the Hebrew women who gave birth. I brought them in, on one of the previous chapters. They were directed to kill the male children and allow the female children to live as they were not considered a threat to Egypt.

Through discernment, these two women were able to figure out the answer they gave to the king when it was discovered that they were not killing the male children as they were instructed and their answers were perfect. The midwives said to Pharaoh, because the Hebrew women are not as the Egyptian women. They are lively and deliver their babies before the midwives come in to them.

From their answer, you can see that they had thought carefully about what they will say in response to the king and asked God to help them. You must understand that it is not easy to appear before a king like Pharaoh and answer his questions without being queried further. He had men of great knowledge and intelligence in his cabinet. But the Bible does not have any record of these women being accused of any wrong doings. It states that God dealt well with the midwives and made them houses.

As Miriam watched intently for who would appear and see her brother, the princess of Egypt herself showed up. In this biblical story, we find that at a very young age, Miriam already had cultivated heaven's gifts in her young life. As she watched the princess open the basket to see a crying baby, the young Miriam boldly approached this daughter of royalty with a plan to care for the baby.

She showed confidence and maturity to be so discerning having been trained well by a mother who led by example. The seeds of hope and deliverance, so long cultivated by her mother were now thriving in her life that even at a young age she was blessed with the gift of discernment.

A person of discernment is always able to accurately read character and motives. Once they understand others, an individual with discernment has the ability to select what is an appropriate response in every situation and circumstances. This is exactly what happened with the youthful Miriam, after discerning the compassion shown by Pharaoh's daughter, she immediately responded by providing a wonderful offer to the princess for the care and nurturing of this Hebrew baby who was her own little brother.

As I said in the previous paragraph, Miriam carried what was transferred to her from her mother. The record, says that when her mother conceived and bore a son, she saw that the child was a goodly child. One might mistake the word goodly, to mean that the child was good looking but that is not what it means in this circumstance.

The woman had seen beyond the limit of an ordinary eye. She discerned in the realm of the spirit, that the boy was a special gift and though she did not understand it, she decided to try and save him and God used this woman to prepare His weapon for the deliverance of His children from Egypt.

It was God that placed Miriam in the place of learning from her mother because she must fulfill her own part in the script that He (God); had written by Himself which His Spirit was personally choosing the characters. The mother and the daughter did not know what they were doing or why they did what they did but the author, who arranged and placed them on each scene, gave them the gift of discernment that at each point, they did what was right.

Who can understand all this but the one that is filled with the Holy Spirit? The whole story of Moses, his mother and sister had been written and the manuscript handed over to the Spirit of God to implement according to the will of God the Father.

Even though Pharaoh killed the male children that were born at that time, Moses must be born. His mother was given the gift of discernment in order to know what to do and save him against all the odds. His sister too received the same gift of discernment to do what she did against all the odds.

Here again is the Shunammite woman. She is included in this list of discerning women. When this woman saw

Elisha, she did not invite him to eat bread in her house for any other reason other than that she perceived that he was a holy man of God.

This word perceive, points to discernment. She discerned that Elisha was a holy man of God and she shared it with her husband demanding that they should make a room in their house for him. It was the Spirit of God at work in her for two purposes. One was to provide an accommodation for Elisha and the other was for her to conceive and bear a child.

She did not know about the second purpose until it came to pass, then she discerned it was also part of it. So at the death of her son, she knowing what God had already done for her; was not ready to confess negatively. She had discerned that the child was a gift for her from God and she knew the gift of God is without repentance. That was why she went to see Elisha and acted the way she did. She showed absolute confidence found only in someone who believes in what God can do.

God did not waste time in reviving this woman's dead son back to life because she was in tune with the Spirit of God.

She had made herself available to be used and was open for information from heaven. This brought about the impartation of discernment on her, to help her in doing the will of God when the time came. You can see that her position as a well to do woman, did not limit her, it rather assisted her in doing what was required to be done and God loved her.

Before I bring up the next woman of discernment, I want you to read these passages taken from the scripture in 1 Samuel chapter 25;

21 Now David had said, surely in vain have I kept all that this fellow hath in the wilderness, so that nothing was missed of all that pertained unto him: and he hath requited me evil for good. 22 So and more also do God unto the enemies of David, if I leave of all that pertain to him by the morning light any that pisseth against the wall.

The above were statements, David made when he was angry over the report brought to him about Nabal's treatment on his men that he had sent to him. The tune of this statement is war and destruction. But someone in the person of Abigail, the wife of Nabal discerned it in advance and quickly made arrangement to avert the coming circumstances.

Again the Spirit of God, who knew the heart of this woman and loved her, was at work to bring her to meet David. Her husband was already scheduled to die and she was to become David's wife.

This brings to light as truth, the statement that God works in mysterious ways. As soon as Abigail came in and was told what happened when the men of David came, she discerned what would happen next and also discerned what she should do. She did not say anything to her husband but instead went to meet David on the way.

If you read down the verses that followed, you will see the statements she made on meeting him and understand the whole scenario as planned by God. What she said to David, were taken from a written manuscript whose writer was God. Her intelligence was exceptional.

Ruth was another woman who read and acted from God's manuscript. How can you describe a young woman's resolve to follow an old woman to her own country? This woman was her mother in-law, yes but her husband was dead and his mother was going away because she had no hope. Naomi's husband was dead with her two sons of which one was Ruth's husband. What future does Ruth have with her? The Bible says that she cried and told her not to tell her, to leave her. I think that was where, she touched God and He loved her.

The Spirit of God got to work fast. Ruth discerned what was beyond the ordinary and was willing to hold on to it. She saw, her future with the old woman. I believe she saw a man holding her hands in marriage in the other country where Naomi was going. She did not know this man, but she also saw that after they were married, she conceived and bore a child. She discerned all these, before their manifestation and said, "I will go where you go". You know the rest of the story.

Let us look at Mary, the mother of Jesus and see the character of discernment she possessed. The word of God says in Luke chapter 1; that in the sixth month the angel Gabriel was sent from God to a city of Galilee, named Nazareth. It was to a virgin espoused to a man whose name was Joseph, of the house of David that this angel was sent and the virgin's name was Mary.

If you ask me what I understand from this reading, I will answer simply by telling you that Mary was a virgin. You ask again, was she the only virgin? I will answer, No and include that she was even espoused to a man named Joseph. You ask further, so why did God send the angel to her? This is difficult to answer but I found help when I read verse 29 of Luke 1;

"And when she saw him, she was troubled at his saying, and cast in her mind what manner of salutation this should be".

Now I can say in answer to the last question that Mary was a special woman to God, who filled her with the Holy Spirit. She was anointed for the purpose she served and the Spirit of God had been following her around until the day the angel came to visit her.

If you look at the story of the birth of Jesus in book of Matthew, you will see that it was God that protected her when Joseph her husband thought of how to put her away.

God did not allow him to do what he had planned. He sent an angel to visit Joseph in a dream and told him, what he needed to hear.

It is the Holy Spirit that gives the gift of discernment. Mary's mind was active. The record says; that when the angel greeted her strangely, she was troubled at his saying and thought in her mind what manner of greeting that was. She tried to discern it by querying the angel further.

That was how she got the full information and before saying, "I am the Lord's servant; may your word to me be fulfilled".

My thought here is that if she had not discerned it to be from God, she would have rejected it. She was a very careful woman who depended on God.

Remember that Mary had a cousin called Elizabeth and I want to bring in this Elizabeth as a discerning woman. How do I mean, you may ask? I will explain after you have read the following verses from the same book of Luke chapter 1 shown below as follows;

41 And it came to pass, that, when Elisabeth heard the salutation of Mary, the babe leaped in her womb; and Elisabeth was filled with the Holy Ghost: 42 And she spake out with a loud voice, and said, Blessed *art* thou among women, and blessed *is* the fruit of thy womb. 43 And whence *is* this to me that the mother of my Lord should come to me? 44 For, lo, as soon as the voice of thy salutation sounded in mine ears, the babe leaped in my womb for joy. 45 And blessed *is* she that believed: for there shall be a performance of those things which were told her from the Lord.

Elizabeth was not with Mary when the angel visited her but you can see how the Spirit of God came upon her and she began to talk about what the angel had told Mary. She discerned the secret things of God through this gift of the Holy Spirit.

The Spirit of God was using her to confirm the word, the angel spoke to Mary and she confirmed it boldly with a loud voice. It was through her statements that Mary was strengthened and encouraged. She immediately burst into singing and magnified the name of the Lord God almighty. I can say that God loved these two women dearly

226

I have talked about Mary Magdalene in virtually all the chapters of this book. Every woman will like to be talked about like her, but her case was an anointing. Jesus said that what she did will be remembered in her memory wherever the gospel is preached all over the world.

What did she do? She broke a bottle of an expensive ointment on the Lord. Now why would she do that on the Lord? She discerned that it was the right thing to do. You can understand it better by reading what Jesus said in the scripture as written in the book of Mark 14: 8 below;

"She hath done what she could: she is come aforehand to anoint my body to the burying".

What she did was ordained by God in order to confirm that Jesus will surly die as He had told His disciples over and over again, but they refused to accept it. The Spirit of God working in this woman used her, by allowing her to discern the art and bringing it to pass.

When this woman and the others went to the grave of Jesus and saw that His body had been taken away, she also discerned that staying there a little while was not a bad idea and she became the first person to see the risen Jesus. What a grace? The truth here is that she made herself available to be used and God loved her.

When the Samaritan woman met with Jesus at the well of water, she said to Jesus; "I perceive that you are a prophet". What prompted this statement is that Jesus told her, her true position as an unmarried woman living with a man that was not her husband.

Right there and then, she began to discern something supernatural and she left as soon as the disciples of Jesus returned to be with him. The record says that she left her water pot and went asking a question that was triggered in her heart by the Spirit of God and that was, "Is not this, the Christ?" Before she know it, she was evangelizing.

This was why the Spirit of God overtook her when she met with Jesus and she fell in love with him. He used her, to evangelize her city and that was better than eating food. When His disciples pleaded with Him to eat, He said, "I have food to eat that you know not of". The joy that was coming to Him as the woman took the good news into the city was overwhelming.

He made the following statements recorded from verses 34-37;

"Jesus saith unto them, My meat is to do the will of him that sent me, and to finish his work. Say not ye, there are yet four months, and then cometh harvest? Behold, I say unto you, Lift up your eyes, and look on the fields; for they are white already to harvest. And he that reapeth receiveth wages, and gathereth fruit unto life eternal: that both he that soweth and he that reapeth may rejoice together. And herein is that saying true, one soweth, and another reapeth".

The woman did the greatest job there is to be done in the whole world and how did she get into it? She discerned the Lord. He also wants you to discern and fall in love with Him.

There is also a certain woman whose name was Lydia, a seller of purple, of the city of Thyatira. This woman heard the word of God spoke by Apostle Paul and discerned it as the true gospel. She was not the only woman there on the day Paul and his team came to her area, but the scripture says that she worshipped God and it was God who opened her heart to hear them.

Jesus said that it is His Father, who attracts those who come to Him and this was exactly what happened here. The Spirit of God worked in her and she received the gift of discernment for the purpose of accepting the true gospel of Jesus Christ. Her story is recorded in the book of Acts chapter 16 as follows:

13 And on the Sabbath we went out of the city by a river side, where prayer was wont to be made; and we sat down, and spake unto the women which resorted thither. 14 And a certain woman named Lydia, a seller of purple, of the city of Thyatira, which worshipped God, heard *us*: whose heart the Lord opened, that she attended unto the things which were spoken of Paul. 15 And when she was baptized, and her household, she besought us, saying, if ye have judged me to be faithful to the Lord, come into my house, and abide there. And she constrained us.

She may have heard about the Lord and worshipped Him so many times, but the day she met Paul and his team, was different. God had been preparing her for a day like that and she discerned it because she desired it in her heart. She looked forward to that day and when it came, she knew it.

She had positioned herself to receive God the day He would visit her, so she was open on this day.

One thing is certain; it is the heart which seeks the Lord that finds Him. He is looking for people with such heart all around the world and you are included. When you worship God in Spirit and in truth, He loves to see the joy He brings into your heart, flowing out to the notice of even your enemies. You will begin to experience something different in your life because it must change to your amazement.

This is the revelation that you have been waiting for. Arise to your feet and get ready to experience a love that no man can give to you. It only comes from the Almighty Father of all creation. It has been Him all the while. He loves you and will continue to carry you on the Eagles wind.

CHAPTER ELEVEN: Interactive Woman

> COME NOW, AND LET US REASON TOGETHER, SAITH
> THE LORD: THOUGH YOUR SINS BE AS SCARLET,
> THEY SHALL BE AS WHITE AS SNOW; THOUGH THEY
> BE RED LIKE CRIMSON, THEY SHALL BE AS WOOL.

Interaction is communication and God loves it. This is different from prayer. It brings you to the awareness of His presence wherever you are and guides your reactions to every issue of life whether at home or outside the home. God always shows love to every woman who interacts with Him. Looking back at all the women I told their stories in this book, you will see that they were women of interaction. None of them got to where they were able to get to, without open interactions.

The word of God says, come let us reason together. This means that God is giving you an opportunity for interaction with Him. He said that He will hear you and make things right no matter how bad you feel they are. Imagine a father who wants to hear and understand you at all the times. He will not raise a finger on you or speak to you harshly. He only wants you to tell Him whatever it is and He will take care of it. That is the kind of father anyone would like to have, isn't it? He also wants you to listen to Him, hear and obey Him.

Interaction solves a lot of the problems of life. Many times, there have been issues that you would have overcome by just talking about it, asking questions or making request for suggestions but you kept them to yourself. By this therefore, you are bearing the pains associated with these things alone thereby offending yourself, offending others and even God. You many times, make issues where there should be no issues just because you refused to interact and you always say that you want to leave it that way. This is always very dangerous and unhealthy.

God frowns at such behaviors. The woman god will love and use, is that woman who opens up. She will not keep to herself when she feels offended, abused, insulted, rejected or treated badly by anyone including God Himself. This woman speaks out in all occasions, expressing her feelings and tries to put things in order. Wherever she needs understanding, she asks questions without fear and whenever she needs guidance, she seeks it cheerfully. This woman never bears any grudge in her heart, for either man or God.

Paul wrote that the head of man, is Christ and the head of the woman is the man. He therefore advised that the woman should interact with her husband. If only Eve had said to that wicked serpent, let me call my husband or she made efforts to ask her husband to explain the serpent's queries on that day, the serpent would not have had its way with her. But there was a communication gap between the husband and his wife and that was what permitted the enemy to take advantage of Eve.

It was Sarah who went to Abraham and told him to take her maid and sleep with her, so that they could have a child through her. This would have been a deep discussion between the husband and the wife. Sarah must have taught it over in the cause of her burden to bear a son for her husband and then she opened up in an interaction with him. When the maid became pregnant and started proving stubborn, Sarah again interacted with her husband and sent her away. God did not interfere in the matter by telling Abraham or his wife anything. He instead sent a messenger to the maid and directed her to return to her madam and be obedient to her.

When Abraham and Sarah went to live in the land of the Gerar, they agreed that Sarah should tell anyone that asked her, that Abraham was her brother and it was so. When Abimelech the king of Gerar sent for Sarah and took her, God came to him in the dream and told him that he was as good as dead because of the woman he took. God again did not blame Abraham and his wife for what they did. Instead, he defended them. The word of God says that if two people shall agree concerning anything, it shall be done for them and agreement is done through interaction.

It was the servant of Abraham that met Rebebak who became the wife of Isaac at the well where she came to get water. First the servant asked her to give him water to drink and she responded. This created an interaction between them and when he asked her whose daughter she was, her response brought solution to the servant's needs. She also told the servant that there was a space for him, in her father's house. You can understand, that she was not aware of the servant's prayer to God but the interaction they had opened doors for her.

Jacob had married the two daughters of a man named Laban and was working for him. There was a time Jacob's life was threatened in the house of his in-law Laban and the Lord told him to go back to the land of his fathers and his relatives. Jacob had to call his wives and interacted with them. He explained their father's attitude towards him and his fears. After their discussions and the details he gave to his wives, they understood him and agreed to leave their father's house with their children. It was through their interactions, that Jacob their husband was able to convince them.

These women I have mentioned so far; could be interacted with because they were open and obedient to their husbands. If there had been any gap between them, they would not have been able to agree with each other. What need is there for you to decided to stay on your own? You may say that it's your life, but you have to understand that you were created for a relationship. You were not created to exist on your own, by yourself and for yourself.

Miriam the sister of Moses saw the daughter of Pharaoh when she found the basket in which her brother Moses was kept in the water. She immediately ran to this woman and opened up an interaction with her and this interaction created a chance for their mother to be brought, to nurse the baby until he grew.

Rahab interacted with the spies who came from Israel to spy on Jericho. As the bible reported it, she was the one who went to the spies before they laid, down for the night and started telling them all she knew about their nation and their God. She further made a request for them to show kindness to her family and the spies responded by giving her the conditions for an agreement to hold between them. They continued to interact until all the terms and condition were accepted and agreed on before the spies left her. She knew that she had to talk and she opened up a discussion which she used to secure herself and her family.

You must understand that the way an interaction is introduced can either make it achieve its purpose or destroy it. The woman, who wants to start an interaction, must therefore try to ensure that she has thought about it carefully. It is always very important, to think it out before implementing it. You must learn to know where to come in at every circumstance and how to start. Understanding the mood of the person you wish to interact with; is also very important. While some interactions can come in at any time, some needs special times or occasion.

The bible did not record that the mother of Samuel told her husband while she was pregnant that she intended to give the child to God. It was after she had delivered and weaning him that she told her husband about her intention. May be she should have told him earlier, but she understood the mood of the man. She knew the right time to tell him and avoid quarrel between them. That kind of interaction was too sensitive.

There was an interaction between Abigail and David on that day she went to meet him on behalf of her husband. She mastered her speech and coordinated herself as she spoke. I wrote in one of the chapters of this book that David was attracted to her by the way she approached him. There was maturity in her approach and the warrior responded with thanking God. Even though David had decided to kill her husband and his family, this woman made him change his mind by talking sweetly to him.

The Shunnammite woman interacted with her husband and told him that she saw a man named Elisha. When she explained to her husband that she believed that this man was a holy man of God and that they should make a room for him in the roof of their house, I am sure that her husband asked her some questions like; how do you know what you are saying is true? How can you suggest that we should make a room in our house for a total stranger? What if he is thief? They argued it until she was able to convince her husband with good points and he accepted her proposal.

Most times, interactions bring about disagreements. But such disagreements are never too difficult to resolve, when there are good points. In fact, it is during necessary disagreements that you can learn and gather more information on a subject matter. Don't say that you don't like disagreements and thereby stay limited. Bring the matter out on the table, discuss it and have a better understanding. Any partnership where there is no disagreement is not real. Someone has something to hide.

At the well in Samaria where Jesus met a woman, the bible record shows that He came there and sat down to rest and wait while His disciples went to buy food. It was when the woman came to get water that He spoke by asking her for water to drink. The woman's answer to Him showed that she had deep information and belief on religion. This was what created an opportunity for the interesting interaction she had with Jesus which brought about her healing.

Reading that story, one could see that the woman had a lot on her mind. She obviously had many questions that she needed answers to. If she had not met Jesus on that day and He spoke to her, she would have continued to live her life the way it was and might have died with all those unanswered questions in her head. You must understand that like this woman, there are others who are carrying too many unanswered questions for which they seek answers inwardly. They speak to themselves and many times murmur in their attempts to get answers.

How can you ask yourself a question and answer it? It is always better to speak out and be heard than to die in silence. When the load is beyond your understanding and you have no capacity to handle it, take it to God. He is your best friend and closest confidant. Don't forget that marriage brought two together, to become one. Therefore the one who is married should not be alone. When there is problem in your marriage, take it to God. He instituted marriage for a purpose and has all the keys to solving every marital issue. Jesus said in John fourteen verse eighteen; "I will not leave you comfortless".

His promise is that He will send you another comforter, who will be with you and He told you His name. Once you become born again and worship God in spirit and in truth, the Holy Spirit becomes your continuous sweet companion. He takes over the affairs of your life and begins to give you guidance in all things. The word of God, show that He (The Spirit of God) will tell you when to turn to the left or to the right. He becomes your friend and will answer all your questions.

I therefore advise you to release yourself from all your burdens and commit it to Him. What it takes, is your opening your mouth to speak. Just say something. No man knows you like you know yourself. You have to call on the one who is the architect of your life, to come to your aid. He knows you even more than you know yourself. Let Him come into your heart and He will assist you. He is by you right now. You can begin to worshipping Him and lift your hands to Him in admiration. He loves dearly.

I remember Martha and Mary in the book of Luke chapter 10. Jesus went to visit the sisters who were dear to Him and while He was there, Martha kept herself busy with running around to serve the Lord. All this time, Mary sat with Jesus and was interacting with Him. At a time, her sister who felt that she should have assisted her in her busyness went to complain to Jesus. She complained to Him that she had been busy in the kitchen since He came but her sister instead of helping her, just sat with Him. Jesus in reply, told her that her sister chose the most important thing. He is waiting to interact with you.

I give a special thanks to Monique. I met her at a campground and this woman became exceptional in my life. She's a gift and truly a sample of the woman God loves. I honestly think I met an Angel because she is everything I have written in this book.

Made in the USA
Middletown, DE
01 March 2022